Debating Modern Revolution

DEBATES IN WORLD HISTORY

Series Editor: Peter N. Stearns, George Mason University, USA

Bloomsbury's *Debates in World History* series presents students with accessible primers to the key debates in the field of world history, from classic debates, such as the great divergence, through to cutting-edge current developments. These are short, argumentative texts that will encourage undergraduate-level history students to engage in the practice of doing history.

PUBLISHED:

Debating the Industrial Revolution, Peter N. Stearns
Debating Modern Revolution, Jack R. Censer

FORTHCOMING:

Debating the Great Divergence, Michael Adas, Joseph Schmidt and Joseph J. Gilch

Debating Modern Revolution

The Evolution of Revolutionary Ideas

JACK R. CENSER

BLOOMSBURY ACADEMIC
LONDON • NEW YORK • OXFORD • NEW DELHI • SYDNEY

BLOOMSBURY ACADEMIC
Bloomsbury Publishing Plc
50 Bedford Square, London, WC1B 3DP, UK
1385 Broadway, New York, NY 10018, USA
29 Earlsfort Terrace, Dublin 2, Ireland

BLOOMSBURY, BLOOMSBURY ACADEMIC and the Diana logo are
trademarks of Bloomsbury Publishing Plc

First published 2016
Reprinted 2016, 2017, 2019, 2021

A catalogue record for this book is available from the British Library.

Library of Congress Cataloging-in-Publication Data

Censer, Jack Richard.
Debating modern revolution : the evolution of revolutionary ideas /
Jack R. Censer.
London : Bloomsbury Academic, an imprint of Bloomsbury
Publishing Plc, 2016. | Series: Debates in world history | Includes
bibliographical references and index.
LCCN 2015030405 | ISBN 9781472589620 (hardback) | ISBN
9781472589637 (paperback) | ISBN 9781472589651 (ePDF) | ISBN 9781472589644
(ePub)
LCSH: Revolutions—History. | Revolutions—Philosophy. |
Revolutionaries—Biography. | World politics—18th century. | World
politics—19th century. | World politics—20th century. | World
politics—1989- | BISAC: HISTORY / Revolutionary. | HISTORY / Modern /
General. | HISTORY / World.Classification: LCC JC491.C376 2016 | DDC 303.6/4—dc23
LC record available at http://lccn.loc.gov/2015030405

ISBN: HB: 978-1-4725-8962-0
PB: 978-1-4725-8963-7
ePDF: 978-1-4725-8965-1
eBook: 978-1-4725-8964-4

Series: Debates in World History

Typeset by Integra Software Services Pvt. Ltd
Printed and bound in the United States of America

In Memoriam

Lenard Berlanstein (1947–2013)

Roy Rosenzweig (1950–2007)

Contents

Illustrations

Figures

Maps

Acknowledgments

Writing a book like this one, with sections across a broad geographical and chronological span, tests the knowledge of any historian working today where specialization is the norm, and I am hardly an exception. To remedy that, I relied on many scholars for assistance, and the George Mason University history faculty were incredibly willing to listen and provide necessary help. Likewise, many friends, among them historians of France, encouraged me to write this book and gave aid as well. I did rely heavily on Gary Kates and Lloyd Kramer who read the entire manuscript at a critical stage. Others who endured numerous conversations and read parts of the manuscript were Rex Wade, Rosemarie Zagarri, Jeffrey Wasserstrom, and Matt Karush. Along the way Michael Chang, Mark Katz, Bassam Haddad, Steve Barnes, Shaul Bakhash, Jack Goldstone, and Brian Platt provided help and needed advice as well as did Jill Bowen and Katie Clare. Rex Wade and Donald Sutherland were enormously supportive throughout the project. And there is no room to thank all those people who were kind enough to listen to my ideas and proffer suggestions.

I would like to thank especially Peter Stearns who has been a supporter over most of my career in many different ways and recruited me to write this book. It has been a great challenge and opportunity to learn something new. Jane Turner Censer, my wife and fellow historian, was absolutely critical to this work, as she has been in every venue of my life. Our children, Marjorie and Joel, always make work and life that much more meaningful. Of course, none of these people are responsible for the information and interpretation in this work: I take full responsibility for those.

Finally, I have dedicated this book to my late colleagues Lenard Berlanstein and Roy Rosenzweig who provided intensive friendship and community framework for most of my working life and who sadly died well before I or anyone else was ready for that loss. On behalf of the many others whose lives and careers they touched, I find it intensely satisfying to thank them for what they have done.

Introduction

Despite much scholarly writing on the history of revolution, including the comparative history of revolutions, the actual ideas that propelled revolutions, as they evolved over time, have received far less consideration. Polemicists have engaged with this subject, largely to decry revolutions, but no focused examination of the idea of revolution in global perspective has emerged. This book, actually an extended essay, therefore endeavors to conceptualize and describe the influential meanings of revolution.

As "revolution" has been used to describe changes not only in politics but also in such areas as society and fashion, what do we mean in studying this term? Here the focus will be on the political but not even all of that. Although many competing definitions denote what constitutes a political revolution, most often it refers to violent changes that start with political events but encourage something broader such as an appreciable social, economic, and cultural alteration in one or more of those arenas. To be sure, Czechoslovakia experienced the nonviolent Velvet Revolution; Nelson Mandela had given up violence long before his efforts helped upset the political and racial regime in South Africa; and Gandhi overthrew British rule (though little else) in India in 1948 through massive protests far more than through violence. Further, some violent political actions do not lead to broader social change, but such events are usually termed coup d'états, not revolutions. Somewhat arbitrarily, this book does not focus on such specific political coups but on violent revolutions that institute highly significant changes. Additionally, one other defining characteristic is that revolutions seek change that contemporaries view as progressive. This seems to me the most debatable boundary of all; yet without it, the topic becomes overly diffuse. Some historians doubt that most revolutions before the eighteenth century were progressive but instead generally sought to restore a real, or imagined, more perfect past world. Leaving aside these "restorations," this book engages political ideas in major revolutions, accompanied by violence and progressive from the contemporaneous point of view, since the eighteenth century. In order to convey the texture of revolutionary thought, this book focuses on a few critical revolutions and emphasizes exemplary ideological issues, placing them in political chronology for context. Also, Karl Marx in the nineteenth century and Frantz Fanon in the twentieth century receive attention to enhance our understanding of major ideological contributions of specific revolutions.

One further issue remains. In the eighteenth century, prior to the American and French revolutions, contemporaries often discussed change without using the word revolution to mean violent, large-scale political change. Thus, the early sections of this book must examine actions that appear to us as part of the revolution to understand what past political leaders meant by revolution even when they used different words for what we now call revolution; and we must consider how others thought about and observed these activities. Understanding these perspectives requires a cultural approach in which we combine ideas, actions, and reactions. The book's methods shift some after the eighteenth century. With prominent revolutions in the immediate past, rebellious individuals in the nineteenth century began to spell out what revolution meant in more self-conscious terminologies. They also spoke directly to large segments of the population which responded and added their own views. Explicit ideas of revolution will become far more prominent in these sections.

Defining revolution as a violent attempt to change values emphasizes the purpose of political actions. Revolutionaries may dwell on the institutions to be replaced, the depredations they have faced, or even the methods that are or are not acceptable. Thus, depending on the specific event, this book also considers subjects well beyond the initial purposes that most indelibly mark a revolutionary movement.

Sharpening the focus does not completely solve the problems of packing so much material into a short book. Consequently, while each chapter describes the arrival of new ideas, I do not mean to suggest that previous notions of revolution perished; in fact they generally did not. Even to this present day, the eighteenth-century democratic revolutions attract many, many adherents. But to explain the competing ideas and give some sense of their substance over time, this book concentrates on the new notions of revolution in succeeding centuries. The actual competition among these different, often contradictory notions could fill another book. For example, early nineteenth-century Paris was alive with an incredible variety of ideas; and over a century later the Cold War witnessed battles between seemingly irreconcilable yet revolutionary ideologies. And one might envision, somewhat tendentiously, an eighteenth-century liberal democratic revolution unseating a decaying Marxist regime.

But this book takes up new beliefs as they emerged in layers, advantaged by considering related revolutions that together provide a sense of the era. The first group, the American and French revolutions, explores the paths to overthrow existing authority—foreign or monarchical—and replaces it with sovereignty invested in the population and expressed through legal equality and political participation. Chapter 2, which chronicles the period from 1800 to 1871, evaluates the South American version of earlier, more northerly events and then examines the arrival of ethnic nationalism, emphasizing the Italian nationalist revolution. Although Marxism generated no revolution during this era, Marx then created his seminal interpretation; and the chapter discusses his views. In this period, revolution added new goals—proletarian revolution and nationalism—but only the latter was widely realized in Italy and throughout Europe.

By focusing on communism and its roots in Marxism, Chapter 3 presents the two really big and determining revolutions of the twentieth century—those of the Russians and the Chinese. Included here was not only a new right—economic equality—but also its extension to nonindustrial societies with the notion of modernizing the economy. Theoretically, sovereignty passed to the laboring classes. Chapter 4 engages the revolutions that shook the world as African and Asian countries emerged from colonial rule, especially after the Second World War. Although some of these revolutions embraced Marxism and called themselves communist, their essential features really moved far away from those of the Russians and even the Chinese. The Vietnamese and Cubans emphasized the importance of the peasants more than their predecessors and thus deserve separate treatment. In addition, this chapter analyzes the ideas of Frantz Fanon, whose writings, while not connected to any particular revolution, had an enormous impact, even on would-be revolutionaries in the West. As expressed by Fanon, anti-imperialism superseded the previous independence movements by greater hostility to the occupying power and its emphasis on exclusion of the colonizers as part of the definition of the sovereign power. Some of his views connect to Marxist revolutionaries.

This intensive examination of Marx and his ideological descendants reflects the copious discussions they sparked among almost everyone who supported or opposed revolutions. In part, because the Marxists wanted to both embrace and revise Marx's ideas, they more openly and clearly developed their changing ideas about their revolutions. This legacy influences the shape of this book. Moreover, at least until recently, Marxist thought was adopted very widely by both revolutionaries and even reformers. But recently, religion—particularly Islam—has become very important in inspiring revolutionaries. Although this book focuses on the Ayatollah Khomeini and the Iranian revolution, his success, his ideas, or both have stirred others—liberals as well as fundamentalists. Thus, this book takes us to the present; moving ahead, no doubt readers can add additional concepts not forecast here as they reconsider the meanings of the idea of revolution.

Political revolution has had a great run, even though it really has been less than perfect. Based on the notion that revolutionary ideas were a new fashion in the late eighteenth century, this book traces these beliefs over four different centuries. Such notions have played a gigantic role in past events. We cannot imagine the current world without reference to the frequent reliance on radical political change. The past may explain the present but not predict it. Nonetheless, as the conclusion argues, until humans give up on perfectibility in this world, revolutions will continue. Understanding this idea of the content of revolutions is valuable alongside the work of other scholars who have focused upon the underlying causes. Adding the global penetration of this idea can only assist understanding.

As part of the book series on global history for the educated readers, *Debating Modern Revolutions: The Evolution of Revolutionary Ideas* attempts not only to synthesize and present in brief a vast subject but also to stimulate further thought and discussion beyond these pages for the general public as well as high school and college students. To that purpose, each chapter at its end includes an "essay" that shows different views of revolution that can be compared and contrasted. Each "essay" includes a question to focus readers, with other such questions scattered throughout the book. This book also provides a short list of readings that can further encourage deeper contemplation. With these additional sources, the essays, and the propositions, readers may extend their learning and confront the many vexing questions posed by revolutions over the last quarter millennium.

1

The Emergence of Modern Theories of "Rights" and the First Modern Revolution

Before the revolutions

Although revolutions had occurred before the eighteenth century, well back in history, and as recently as seventeenth-century England, eighteenth-century people in practice did not consider the possibility of this recourse. So foreign to their minds was the term "revolution" that the word in French denoted only movements like the planets around the sun or more relevantly a new minister or king replacing a predecessor. While the English continued to celebrate their "Glorious Revolution" of 1688, many scholars have come to view it as glorious because it was no revolution at all, but a restoration to the status quo ante. The eighteenth-century English tended to ignore the genuine revolution, as defined here and carried out by Cromwell in the 1650s. Thus, on top of a pointed forgetfulness, there was a serious gap between 1688 and the American Revolution, a separation in time and intensity that justifies starting this book in the eighteenth century.

Although most of the eighteenth century witnessed neither revolution nor revolutionary movements, considerable political turbulence existed. In fact, two outstanding interpretations of

Western and global politics, by Robert Palmer and Franco Venturi, clearly found revolution occurring seldom, sporadically, and only twice successfully at the end of the era—in the British colonies and France. Palmer, in two magnificent volumes published in 1959 and 1964, asserted that more tension generally emerged when an aggressive, rising aristocracy confronted monarchs who had primarily spent the previous century enlarging kingly power. Describing political systems, primarily European, he emphasized that despite the enormous consolidation of royal authority, a wide variety of intermediate institutions—parliaments, diets, parlements (law courts), and lots more—formed the basis of aristocratic, and sometimes more popular, opposition. These conflicts, however fraught, seldom had a revolutionary aim to overthrow the current form of government. As efforts to renegotiate, rather than end, the mixed system of royal sovereignty, the opposition intended that the king would return considerable authority to lesser political authorities, mainly dominated by elites.[1]

In a different analysis, Venturi, like scholars in English and North American history, perceived the rising political conflict in the eighteenth century as an ideological struggle between the king and a "country" party. Many who criticized royal power believed that the virtues of the countryside resided in the populace rather than in a corrupt court. This ideology asserted that a right of resistance sprang from the customary rights of Englishmen, who had long been guaranteed limits on royal power by the Magna Carta as a founding document. Even before the Stamp Act crisis, Americans with their own grievances also resorted to this same ideology to resist George III. Like Palmer, Venturi believed that in both these cases, as in a very wide variety of European countries, eighteenth-century people did not imagine a revolution but instead hoped for a rebalancing of power relationships. They might use historic instead of customary to describe their rights but meant roughly the same thing. Englishman John Locke (1632–1704) had laid out a potent personal theory of liberty, representative government, and legal equality; yet no movement followed until decades after his death.

These two snapshots of Europe in mid-century revealed a "revolution free" world in which change mainly figured as an adjustment or even a return to a pristine past. Yet at the end of the last quarter of the eighteenth century, a number of "revolutionary" attempts with new progressive aspects had occurred. The next section scrutinizes the American and French revolutions for several reasons, first and foremost because they were the first to be successful. Particularly important, these revolutions set a world standard followed by later generations. The first revolution occurred in the English thirteen colonies, which Europe already viewed as a wholly different place and a somewhat utopian site. Furthermore, the reliance on a form of "country" ideology (or as it is most often called in this particular geographic context, "commonwealth man") made its success directly relevant to many other countries with similar ideological backgrounds. But the French Revolution was even more obvious as a focus. Eighteenth-century France was the most powerful state in the West, if not in the entire world. Moreover, its revolution was a deeper, more complicated matter as the country became a laboratory for a succession of new political styles. Beginning with constitutional monarchy, the French experimented with representative democracy, direct democracy, dictatorship, and a security state as well as other innovations. Here we shall highlight the early transformative change adopted by the French.

These two events will allow us to observe revolution and the ideas that emerge from both. As a reminder, while later revolutionaries stood on the backs of their eighteenth-century predecessors, knew the course and ideals of revolutions, and often wrote about and planned revolution, eighteenth-century Americans and the French as well, did not know the future and did not set out to make revolutions in a self-conscious way. We have to discern their revolutionary ideals from actions as well as expressions of ideology and culture.

The background for both revolutions must include the Enlightenment alongside country ideology. As this movement had no organization, boundaries, or referees, it remains elusive, almost impossible to define precisely. As the concept of human rights frames both revolutions and is inscribed on their founding documents, we can focus on the background of this concept out of the more general primordial soup of intellectual change.

In contrast to a traditional belief in an active, omnipresent God, a political system dominated by a monarch who held his throne by divine right, and historic rights for subjects, skeptics gradually argued, beginning in the late seventeenth and early eighteenth centuries, for a commitment to empiricism and a creator God not active in everyday life. All of this led toward a more secular world view. Although this deism left God to be the first cause and therefore doubted miracles, it still equated the deity with positive goodness and the universe ordered in a divine way. Empiricism could discover this Godly plan in nature to guide human action. From that basis sprang a belief in human rights as part of, or the best part of, God's benevolence and handiwork. Mankind was not only good but deserving of divinely sanctioned personal freedoms.

At first, human rights were seldom applied to the general political order. As Lynn Hunt has clearly shown, the early evidence for a change was in the growth of empathy.[2] Voltaire's efforts to seek justice for an unfairly executed Protestant enormously enhanced his reputation. Likewise he and the reclusive Jean-Jacques Rousseau—both hardly revolutionaries—could not avoid associating themselves with the progressive forces in Geneva where both resided. In fact, so strong was the surge in empathy for common people that by the end of eighteenth century in Old Regime France, public executions began to draw more sympathy for the condemned than provide a salutary example for the populace. For example, the execution of Damiens, who had tried to assassinate Louis XV in 1757, was so grisly and reaction so strong, that authorities began to close such executions to the public gaze. Even during the revolution, the guillotine aroused sympathy for its victims.

Human rights as an abstract principle for a political order had existed before the revolution. Most famously, John Locke had already articulated this view in the 1690s, but whether he meant human rights or the rights of Englishmen remains unclear. While Rousseau's *Social Contract* embraced equality of rights, those rights seem to be restricted to men. Perhaps more restricted still, the exercise of such rights in his view depended on a small, highly ethical, homogeneous society. Ironically he recommended Corsica, Napoleon's home island. The Emperor must have had a good laugh when he considered Rousseau's view about Corsica's homogeneity in comparison to the intense clan rivalries that Napoleon had experienced.

Secularism, natural law, and a notion of human rights joined "country" theory as well as absolutism (a divinely ordained, and often "absolute" monarchy) in the prerevolutionary mix. While scholars have long debated how the Enlightenment emerged and have offered countless explanations, it is worth noting that one line of thought has focused on interactions with non-Western civilizations. As early as 1935, Paul Hazard, an eminent scholar of the Enlightenment, argued that in the seventeenth century, contact with other civilizations was unsettling to received truths. Hazard noted that encountering different customs challenged the Europeans, who wrote that: "We let our hair grow and shave our faces," but "The Turks shave their heads and grow beards on their faces ... There's no arguing about the right or the wrong of these .... Who is right? Who wrong?"[3] Even more challenging was the discovery of Native Americans, who were not mentioned by the Bible. From this quandary emerged the concept of the noble savage who, next to Europeans, was "... how noble in comparison! His very ignorance is an asset. Unable either to read or write, what a host of evils he escapes! For science and the arts are the parents of corruption." Even while patronizing, Europeans were learning humility and accepting challenge. In fact, asserted Hazard, "The change-over from repulsion to sympathy" was quickly accomplished, influencing not only European beliefs but the empathy that provided the base of shared human rights.[4]

Later, Abbé Raynal in his very influential *History of the Two Indies* (1770), which surveyed much of the non-European world, used the notion of the "other" as a way to critique the "West." This voluminous work, which included contributions by Denis Diderot and other philosophes, attacked despotism and advanced the notion that rebellion against oppression was legitimately a right both inalienable and natural. In addition to its blatant anticlericalism, *History of the Two Indies* emphasized the simplicity and contentment of non-Westerners. Yet that work also pulled its punches. While attacking slavery, the book treated it as a necessary evil that should become more humane. Apparently holding back Raynal and his collaborators was a commitment to property and riches. They made many attacks but treated actual sitting governors with respect. Nevertheless, more than any other work, this book seems to herald revolutionary attitudes, especially in its advocacy of rebellion. Rights propelled revolution but were not universally granted to all.

Fiction too deployed the notion of the nobility of non-Western people, perhaps sincerely, perhaps simply as a perch from which to criticize and deploy Enlightenment notions. For example, Voltaire's *Candide* found Europe a smoldering place full of wars and inhuman acts, while he located El Dorado where noble and upright inhabitants completely ignored the land's abundant gold as they created the most hospitable of worlds. Although most often associated with "country" theory, Montesquieu in his epistolary *Persian Letters* used the naïveté of the non-Western visitors to critique numerous aspects of Old Regime France as well as Europe in general. Published anonymously, but still cautiously, Montesquieu did not directly attack the monarchy but employed an ingenious approach. As the Persian travelers spend more and more time away from their country, the harem implodes. The "eunuchs," intended to ensure the women's purity, seduce them; and all falls apart. One can visualize the readers nodding approval at the revolt of the harem, a barbaric practice by Christian standards. Yet the harem is also transparently a political metaphor which also revealed to Western readers the power of liberty and inhumaneness of a lack of freedom.

Thus, the Enlightenment prepared a script for revolutionaries to use, but it focused more on moral and epistemological changes and reform than on a radical political transformation. These ideas shared the stage with political struggles around the crown and society for reforms. Venturi clearly indicated that, in fact, the most robust challenges occurred from 1755 to 1765; then the initiative mainly passed back to monarchs from 1765 up to 1789—with the notable exceptions of America and France.

The American Revolution

The notion of revolution, or even a serious departure from the association with Great Britain, would have been foreign to the North American colonies at the end of the French and Indian War (known in Europe as the Seven Years War) in 1763. Although influenced by country ideology as well as the Enlightenment, Americans were vigilant but not rebellious.

But all that changed in the 1760s. Even earlier the tight bonds of America and England had been stretched by the movement of settlers from the East Coast into lands where imperial power was weak. The retreat of other European nations that had formerly regulated relationships increased social autonomy and religious innovation.

In the face of all these challenges, the British government felt it had to enhance its highly decentralized form of government. Successive ministries in the 1760s tried various methods to organize and administer the huge accretion of land west of the Appalachians, where white settlers and Native Americans competed. Domestic issues in Great Britain further complicated matters as the new King George III tried in the face of a more restive population to find ministers to suit him.

The French and Indian War (1756–1763) had compounded problems by creating an enormous debt. In fact, prior to 1764–1765, Parliament had never directly taxed its colonies in North America. Although Parliament had, since the time of the English Civil War, passed navigation acts regulating trade, the colonies had basically been allowed to govern their own internal affairs. Each colony had its own legislative assembly to which eligible voters (white males with property) elected representatives. When a colony needed funds, the governor would request that the assembly levy taxes. Even during the French and Indian War, Parliament, requiring funds from the colonists, requested that assemblies tax their inhabitants.

But after the war, new policies emerged. Britain also needed funds to support the upkeep of 10,000 troops which it continued to station on the American frontier. Seeking new sources of revenue, Britain turned to the colonies. Beginning with the Sugar Act of 1764, and continuing with the Stamp Act of 1765 and the Townshend Acts of 1767, Parliament unilaterally imposed a series of taxes on the colonists. These actions violated one of the most cherished rights of Englishmen, the right to be taxed only by legislatures in which they were represented.

By levying such taxes, even as the American economy was reeling, Parliament ignited a firestorm and created huge popular resistance. Although the American newspaper publishers were wary of involvement, the public outcry beginning in 1765 gradually pushed them forward. Riots broke out all over the country. Matters worsened in 1766 when the Parliament repealed the Stamp Act but then passed the Declaratory Act, which allowed it to legislate for the colonies in all matters. Using the term "Declaratory" increased the crisis further as "declaring" in itself implied a strong assertion of power. In this tax-centered confrontation, resistance formed, further intensified by the use of troops to suppress the colonies, with the Boston massacre in 1770 the apogee of repression. Following this event, a deceptive quiet prevailed until 1773 with passage of the Tea Act, which gave the East India Company exclusive privilege to sell the leaf in America. Americans reacted by dumping a shipload of tea into Boston harbor, and the ministry responded with vigor, increasing the number of British troops in Boston.

After the Boston Tea Party, Parliament passed the Coercive Acts. Among other things, these acts voided the Massachusetts charter and chipped away at the inhabitants' right to self-government. Instead of isolating Massachusetts (as Parliament believed it would), the acts rallied those in other colonies to unite against Britain. They believed that if Parliament could take away self-government in one colony, it might soon do so in the others. As the harshness of the Coercive Acts of 1774 became apparent, more and more colonists questioned Parliament's authority and claimed that only the monarch, who had originally issued their colonial charters, possessed authority over them. This corresponded with a shift in thinking about rights. Previously, colonists had appealed to Britain in an effort to preserve their liberties as British subjects. But as it became increasingly clear that Britain continued to ignore their protests and enact new laws that violated their rights, the colonists turned to other justifications for resistance. Instead of defending their rights as Englishmen, they began to insist that Britain was infringing on their "natural rights," rights to life and liberty that were not particular to a specific people or place but that were possessed by all human beings. The invocation of natural rights immensely raised the ideological stakes. Moreover, local colonial politics soon saw heightened involvement from working people, ethnic groups, and an independent press. Ideas of liberty circulated, even though some gentlemen and future Loyalists thought the involvement of these marginal groups objectionable. Liberty as a human right began to gain momentum.

Hostilities brought this confrontation to a head. Fighting around Boston in the spring of 1775 led the Second Continental Congress, already convened in 1775, to establish an army and take control of resistance. Differences escalated so that independence seemed very possible. Thomas Paine expressed the rage of Americans and crystallized intellectual developments, as his pamphlet, *Common Sense*, was written, not for elites, but for artisans, laborers, and agricultural workers, already quite literate by the standards of the day.

In such an environment the Continental Congress chose to issue the Declaration of Independence, not only as a defense of putative historical rights but also from the point of view that Americans had a right to a responsive government because "All men are created equal." This incantation of a universal human right, as a political justification, had become possible only in the last years preceding the Declaration of Independence through the politicization of the populace, the British failure to respond to complaints, and the outbreak of warfare. The Enlightenment had provided this language; the Americans only needed a chance to use it politically. This act, more than Lexington and Concord, proved to be the enduring event heard around the world.

Moreover, abuses of customary rights also provided reasons for leaving the crown and substituting the "people of these colonies" as possessing the right to independence. With sovereignty transferred to the populace, the Declaration claimed specific rights, like the right to wage war, make peace, create commercial taxes, and in general "do all other acts and things which Independent States have right to do." Posterity might also note that the use of the plural "states" here and in the previous sentences would leave the door open to the independence of individual states, the Civil War, and countless other jurisdictional disputes. To be fair, the Declaration also used the term "United" as well.

The Declaration also invoked specific historical rights on which the Americans had previously relied. In fact, a long list of grievances that detailed the monarch's abridgment of historical rights followed more general claims. These two justifications held different bases—history and universal rights—but they were cousins in the opposition to the monarch who abused them. In fact, it is likely that the division of these discourses used by modern scholars was little evident to most Americans or Westerners (with some prominent exceptions such as John Adams), who floated back and forth between these justifications.

But, as it was "human rights" that would proliferate globally, we need to understand more about the founders' document beyond Jefferson's axiom regarding equality. While much of the piece indicted George III and his government in largely "country terms," the first long paragraph established a new nation on the basis of natural law and human rights. With a logic that later became familiar, the document, mainly written by Thomas Jefferson, set as axiomatic that the laws of nature and "Nature's God" (making God a creator more than a current actor), emboldened Americans to dissolve the relationship with England. And Jefferson continued, "all men are created equal" and thus have certain "inalienable Rights," given by God, to possess "life, liberty, and the pursuit of happiness." From these rights flowed appropriate governments, whose power came from the "consent of the governed." If a government violated this bond with its citizens, they could alter it or abandon it in order to benefit from the well-being under a government based on natural law and responsive to its constituents. Moreover, when a government was so despotic as to destroy the rights of man, society had the duty to "throw off such government." This justification certainly did not describe the subservient role of the subject under monarchy. Although England allowed the people historic rights, Jefferson was not just cashing in those rights; instead he was also relying on the universal equality of man to justify "throwing" off English rule. It no longer would be a simple rebalancing of shared political roles. Gloriously eschewing the term revolution, he joined his colleagues to make one.

As independence approached, the Continental Congress coordinated the war against Britain and formally linked the colonies together into a union. Nonetheless, each colony (soon to be state) continued to insist on a considerable autonomy. In 1776, just prior to issuing the Declaration of Independence, Congress requested that the provisional legislatures produce a written document that described in detail the structures, institutions, and procedures by which each state would govern itself after independence. Many also included declarations of rights that described the basic rights and privileges which were held to be fundamental and inviolable. By considering the bills of rights together, one can reach a broader understanding of the colonial mind-set. Eleven of the thirteen states wrote new documents, and these declarations uniformly embraced god-given human rights as a justification for the new governments. With that beginning, they dwelt longest on two subjects, both of which conform to the combination of country ideology with human rights: ensuring that governments would be responsible to the governed and that trials would be fair and by peers.

The historic contest between the British and the colonists clearly led to articulating the first group of customary rights about responsive government but included some natural rights as well. Having been denied the rights of representation that they believed adhered to Englishmen, the Americans made sure that the new governments, based on a different philosophical basis, would include rights that they had been denied. The cornerstone for these claims was the repeated assertion that sovereignty belonged to the people, and some documents called for universal male suffrage. By allowing all males to vote, the Americans were transforming historic rights by making them adhere in nature—at least to the male's nature. In addition, the lawmakers provided both guidance and specific recommendations for the populace to control legislators. Constitutions advised that the common good should be the goal of laws. And legislators ought to be held accountable, by frequent elections and frequent assembly so that ills would not remain unaddressed. One state indicated that all citizens might personally address the legislature. Further, no exclusive privileges could be legislated, and several demanded the separation of powers to rein in overweening lawmakers.

When the English prime minister Lord North sought to subdue the colonies, he suspended some of their customary procedures of justice, particularly the normal venue for complaints about royal officials serving in the colonies. The state bills of rights sought to reaffirm the basic system of justice that colonists had known as British subjects, but this time based it on universal rights, not the historical accident of place of birth. Specifically, bills of rights advocated impartial justice, no self-incrimination, no warrant-less seizures, trial by jury, and sentencing that fit the crime. Also, several demanded an end to excessive bail.

The states universally endorsed freedom of the press, claiming it was necessary as "a great bulwark of liberty" (VA). Or as in Massachusetts: "...liberty of press is essential to the security of freedom in a state ...." Strangely, most documents did not include freedom of speech. By failing to mention this but keeping press liberty, freedom of speech seemed to mean public speech more than spontaneous remarks by individuals. Yet rights of petition were maintained; and the franchise was broad. Political and commercial papers sprang up. The framers of these documents likely had in mind both the customary channel of politics and spontaneous interventions dependent in part on equal rights.

But human rights that could substantiate or at least strengthen these customary ones were also included, even personal liberty. Freedom of religion was guaranteed, however, with restrictions that also showed limits. Some states revealed ambivalence as they specifically granted such freedom only to Christians. Others clearly intended that all citizens must attend church. In fact, Massachusetts specified that "it is the right, as well as the duty of all men in society publicly, and at the stated seasons, to worship the Supreme Being." Adding that this worship cannot disturb "public places," the authors further clarified that "Christians" would be protected by law. Does this imply that non-Christians would not be protected? In addition, many documents indicated a particular personal virtue necessary to preserve these rights of man. In fact, most bills of rights specifically listed as necessary individual traits: "piety, justice, temperance, industry, and moderation." Clearly Christians were favored and church attendance too. Interestingly, personal freedom was to be limited to those who by their self-restraint would not much use it.

Dotting these documents were other elements of customary rights regarding the organized armed force. They frequently expressed opposition to a standing army as well as mentioning the need for control by civilians and for citizens to be armed for the common defense. These words seconded the control of the government by the citizens. Important nuances stand out. First, Pennsylvania and nearby Delaware both allowed individuals to pay for a military substitute. The Delaware document declared: "Nor can any man that is conscientiously scrupulous of bearing arms in any case be justly compelled thereto if he will pay such equivalent." This, like Pennsylvania's exclusion from military service, seems to have been motivated by sympathy for pacifist believers such as Quakers, Moravians, and others. Accompanying this serious protection of the individual's religious conscience were the statements that the purpose of arming individuals was to enable militia service. And this focus may have been quite intentional. Although Vermont was not yet a state, it was restive as a part of New York. Consequently in constructing their own constitution in 1777, Vermonters included a bill of rights that specified that citizens should be armed for their own personal defense as well as for service. This specification acknowledged indirectly that the right had not necessarily included self-defense and guaranteed instead that for Vermont at least, the bearing of arms could be for personal defense. But overall, the principle enunciated the new dependence of the government on citizens for defense instead of a standing army. Furthermore, these states specified the powers of government in their constitutions and separately enumerated some human rights, but did not, on the other hand, generally list the civic obligations of citizens—except for the common defense. This focus underlines the import of Vermont's precise exceptional wording for arming the citizenry and suggests its omission elsewhere was intentional.

The bills of rights also spoke loudly through their omissions, and, like the prejudicial remarks that favored Christians, tended to reduce the declarations' commitment to equality. When they mentioned gender, they mainly intended men. Sometimes, this term was clearly meant to include all people, as in the protection of worship. But in the case of voting, some states listed women and slaves as not included. But not all of the silences should be interpreted as exclusion. New Jersey opened the franchise to women until 1807. Three states allowed free blacks to vote. And in fact scholars have noted that silences also allowed slaves and women later to argue that these rights applied to them. And of course, the pride and universalistic tone of the Declaration of Independence that spills over into these state bills of rights both attracted and spoke to interests of women and enslaved people and other unacknowledged groups. These ambiguities were gradually resolved in favor of white men, who by the 1820s monopolized the electorate. Yet hope lived on for women in the U.S. Constitution, which did not until the Fourteenth Amendment (1868) explicitly equate citizenship with being male.

Thus, by endorsing popular control of and participation in government and a modicum of freedom of speech and religion, the state constitutions undoubtedly underlined in a tempered way much of the Declaration of Independence's enthusiasm for universal rights as well as the rights of the country, "of Englishmen" who were now Americans. Mainly, the government lay under public control, and human rights to individual freedom and equality were intended. However, Americans, once this process was complete, spent little time revisiting these issues in subsequent years. Fighting the revolutionary war and running the states became prime considerations. The Articles of Confederation scarcely mentioned rights. Only the adoption of the Constitution over a decade later revived this issue. The passage of the U.S. Bill of Rights in 1791, two years after the U.S. Constitution, showed that rights were no longer at the forefront. The Constitution, which was an effort to counteract the near anarchy of the interim of the Confederation (1783–1789), instituted a fairly substantial central government whose emphasis on rights mainly concerned political limits on the central government alone rather than the exercise of individual human rights. Ensured was freedom from oppression more than the pursuit of liberty and happiness. Further, slavery was tacitly recognized. Women were not enfranchised and the power of elites through the indirect election of presidents and senators was magnified. In fact, some customary rights were attacked. By passing the Alien and Sedition Acts (1798), the Adams administration undermined political dissent, although Jefferson let these lapse. Many antebellum southern states sought to prevent abolitionist texts from coming in the mail, and northern reporters were intimidated until the 1860s and even later. It would be decades before the tendencies reversed, mainly by amendments to the Constitution after the Civil War and the First World War and Supreme Court decisions of the twentieth century. These later revisions did, in fact, often embrace human rights and maintain their historical place.

Nonetheless, the colonists must be credited with the first successful revolution that implemented a new scheme of government which was justified by history and by the adoption of universal human rights, defined to include personal liberty and political participation, though limited by gender and property qualifications. Whatever the real limits of this promise, this first revolution included the new goals, defended and enabled by the colonists' willingness to employ violence against the British. Not only did Americans make a mark in the sand, but their example decisively contributed to modern definitions of the term revolution: claims to overturn existing governments in the name of the sovereign people, distinctive national traditions, and universal human rights.

How can one explain the states' and nation's drift away from human rights? While many reasons exist for this, the uneasy relationship between the two types of rights is partly responsible. Although the founders did not envision them as incompatible, customary rights are essentially preservationist of individualist prerogative while human rights create the equal populace necessary for the nation's sovereignty. In a country divided by slavery, human rights receded before the customary ones that enable citizen control of the government by dominant groups which could impose their will. From the Civil War on, however, both kinds of rights have had their advocates with dominance ebbing and flowing with the political winds.

The French Revolution: The Old Regime

While the French Revolution followed the American, contemporaries found the former much more important. America, viewed as a savage yet pristine land, provided an ambiguous example, not really relevant to the older, more mature yet corrupt European societies. Thus, the French Revolution held more obvious consequences for older societies. Revolutionaries, in particular, looked to the French Revolution for inspiration, and even well into the twentieth century France was a very important stop on their itineraries. Also, the French Revolution was far more complex because it, in the revolutionary decade (1789–1799), ploughed through at least three distinct phases and several hybrid ones. How it occurred remains hotly debated after more than two centuries.

Kings seated in Paris had ruled for nearly a millennium. From a small region around Paris, they had extended by the eighteenth century their dominion to include territories that altogether resembled modern France. Beginning with a hodgepodge of lands with different feudal governments, they had not only unified the country on paper but in reality too. Although local languages persisted, French was the national language spoken and written in governmental and judicial matters. And from a bureaucratic perspective, eighteenth-century kings could rely on the most extensive, responsive, and best organized governmental structure that had ever existed, at least since France became a large country. Borders were reasonably secure, and a much strengthened police force protected domestic travelers. France had the largest population of any European country and the largest economy too. In population, Paris was second only to London among European cities, and France was a preeminent military power with widespread colonial holdings in the New World and further aspirations. Despite France's losses in the recent Seven Years War, contemporaries still viewed France as intimidating; and in matters of taste, style, and intellectual sophistication, France held unquestioned preeminence. French was the intellectual language, even the required language, at many European courts.

Nevertheless, as in any complex society, dissent existed; and France had many long-term problems. Scholars for over a century have been explaining how the social cleavages in France, particularly the growth of the bourgeoisie or upper middle class, led to the overthrow of a failed regime of aristocratic privilege. Newer scholarship has shown that whatever the anxieties of bourgeois French people, their main goal as they grew wealthy was not to destroy the upper class but to join it. Scholars have been much more persuasive, however, in arguing that class distinctions made a difference once the revolutionary crisis had begun. The second most popular explanation for the Revolution has been that troublesome ideas—country ideology and the Enlightenment—simply caused the French to lose faith in the Church and state and then replace it. Unfortunately, the leading supporters of the philosophes were elites who, however much they favored its ideology, tended to ignore the practical impact of the critiques that related to them. They always favored reform for someone else. Doubtless, the intellectual movements had a huge indirect impact undermining religion and traditional political forms, but before the revolution, at least in France, it is difficult to find fundamental political changes. In fact, in many ways the monarchy used various structures to manage these political problems. The

Enlightenment, economic problems, and social tensions required mobilization to become elements of a revolution. While France had significant social problems of many kinds that may have been growing and political conflicts increasingly divided the king and parlements, only in the revolutionary cauldron did these problems create sustained turbulence and political change.

Consequently, this interpretation relies mainly on the relatively independent logic of politics as the main venue to collect problems and turn them into revolution. Scholars once considered a focus on political narrative, regarded as charting an epiphenomenon, to be extremely unfashionable. Politics were nevertheless very important, as we can see by briefly examining the reign of Louis XV (1715–1774) and at greater length that of Louis XVI (1774–1792).

Unfortunately for Louis XV, he succeeded Louis XIV, the Sun King, whose legacy was decidedly mixed. Although Louis XIV had rescued the crown from its depths of weakness following the Fronde, created political stability, ushered in a glittering court at Versailles, and executed a successful strategy of expansion in the early part of his reign, overspending and an endless succession of wars had by the turn of the eighteenth century undermined his legacy. In short, after a turbulent regency, Louis XV began his reign in 1723 under something of a cloud. Yet, under the chief minister Cardinal Fleury, discord was low; and in 1737 France won a short war that brought it the province of Lorraine. But the rest of the regime was consumed by losses in war, particularly the War of Austrian Succession (1740–1748) and the Seven Years War (1754–1763). The government's main issues (apart from finances) appeared in the three major problems: failed wars, political–religious discord, and moral decay at the court.

Yet to assume that a simple slide into a revolutionary crisis occurred would overlook several aspects. First, this confrontation involved mainly the claims of the traditional rights of the Parlement, rather than the more expansive demands for human rights that became so important in 1789. Furthermore, at first, newly crowned Louis XVI (the late monarch's grandson) and Marie-Antoinette enjoyed a period of genuine popularity. They seemed young and vigorous, seeking a new start away from the venal swamp of Louis XV's Versailles. More important, Louis XVI abolished the new court system established in 1770 to punish the Parlements and brought back the former jurists.

While in the long run this held enormous political consequences, in the immediate case the young monarch appeared far more benevolent than his predecessor. And, in fact, this move positioned Louis as more enlightened than despotic.

Moreover, the king brought in the progressive Anne-Robert-Jacques Turgot as chief finance minister. Associated with the Enlightenment, Turgot urged liberalizing the French economic system and immediately proposed a number of popular measures that earned favor from the general public. In particular, the reforms abolished the guilds of Paris and the *corvée*, an onerous requirement for peasants to contribute their unpaid labor to tending the roads of their area. Although these measures backfired as the parlements blocked them and thereby revealed Louis's political immaturity, they did show the new regime's intent.

Perhaps Louis XVI's reputation was most enhanced by his decision in 1778 to support the revolt of the American colonies. Of course, the main reason for this was geopolitical revenge for the recent loss to Britain in 1763, and the government recognized the ideological risk for an ancient kingdom that backed a republic in revolt against a fellow monarch. So concerned were French officials that they never permitted the state-controlled newspapers to publish the text of the Declaration of Independence and, probably none of the state constitutions described above. Of course, these documents became known through other publications, but the government's unwillingness to abet this process indicated how wary were officials of these ideas. Yet, for once, the French were clearly on the popular side, and the government explained its role, not as supporting revolution, but as assisting a people under the cruel thumb of despotism.

Even more important, the Americans and French were triumphant. Finally the French monarch had won a major war. Victories always earned significant credit, all the more because of the drought in previous years.

The French Revolution—The 1780s

Despite these early successes, more angry voices hostile to the status quo soon were raised. In particular, Marie-Antoinette's popularity rapidly diminished and was replaced by a caricature. Historians have speculated about the causes. Contemporaries found her brazen and too independent, testing gender norms and perhaps appearing sexually dangerous. Feminist scholars have concluded that such criticism was unfounded, based only on the sexist conventions that denied women independence. In fact, some have suggested that the Enlightenment itself, with its emphasis on nature and natural determinism, strongly endorsed sexism. One might add that Louis XVI, undeniably the only Bourbon faithful to his wife but lampooned for his problems in producing an heir, might have inadvertently contributed to the negative view of his bride. Apparently his infertility or lack of sexual vigor was also her responsibility. In any case, even during the Old Regime, the public became massively critical of Marie Antoinette, and scandals and persecution by pornographers increased these problems. Nonetheless, matters could have been worse as the government managed to suppress the lion's share of the most critical pamphlets emanating from English publishers producing the most scurrilous attacks.

But turning this loss of royal reputation into a focused revolution required a specific political crisis, and this came in the form of a budget deficit. This ongoing financial crisis along with the many mounting ideological, social, and bureaucratic issues led to an unsolvable political–economic impasse.

The deficit sprang from debts rung up during the War of Austrian Succession—and later conflicts. Although previous eighteenth-century wars had been paid for, later wars created a particularly large debt. As the economy was only modestly growing through the second half of the eighteenth century, France could not retire the previous borrowings. Concerned by the rising debt, which would be later accelerated by the French intervention in the War of the American Revolution, the government turned in 1776 to Jacques Necker, who was already renowned as an able administrator. And, in fact, by borrowing some 350 million livres, he seemed to earn that confidence. As he convinced the elite and the "public" that all was well, Necker loaded on more and more debt, at very high interest rates. So effective was his propaganda that even despite this, he could continue forward. But his enemies leaked the financial reality, and out of unbelievable presumption, he requested a higher position and suggested difficult reforms that presumably would balance the budget. This gall led to his departure in 1782. Successors followed over the next five years but with similar result.

By 1787, royal fortunes had reached the point of no return; the efforts over the next two years approached nonviolent revolution as absolutism would give way to a modestly limited monarchy: a victory for a rebalancing of royal and elite authority along the shared lines that "country" ideology called for. And it continued. The controller-general Brienne, having failed with a special assembly, engaged Parlement. Louis XIV had forbidden remonstrances;[5] the Parlement in the eighteenth century had forced a return to this practice and had, even before the 1780s, asserted rights based on history to stand guard against monarchical despotism. At times parlements even claimed to "represent" the nation. The Parlement's vision rested on a change in French political culture that worsened relations with the kings of the eighteenth century, which now were extraordinarily poor. In fact, the Parlement's claim to represent the nation was revolutionary itself as it presumed the existence of a national not royal sovereignty. Traditionally, the country had been a collection of entities that only came together in the person of the monarch. But a panoply of developments, most recently described by historian David Bell, had created a national feeling that unified the French. Relevantly, a national press had treated news in national terms and the notion of French public opinion had come into existence.

This new notion of sovereignty was aborning, as the Parlement led and insisted, first and foremost, that the Estates General would be called. Considerable disagreement existed about what this body was, since it had not met since 1614, but contemporaries generally believed it to be an elected body with power over the purse. Public opinion rallied behind the effort of the Parlement. However, when the details were approved on September 25, 1788, the Parlement had approved the traditional form that each estate would vote separately. This meant the clergy (potentially dominated by the upper clerics who belonged to the aristocracy) and the nobility had one vote each, while the Third Estate—the commoners (over 95 percent of the population)—also had one vote. The Parlement had confirmed that the voting configuration that so favored the nobility would not be altered; thus, the "nation," such as it was, would be greatly unrepresented. This exclusion made latent social differences highly problematic.

The clamor from the Parlementary decision on the structure of the Estates General changed everything, because even if the ideas of human rights and broad political participation were dispensable or negotiable to political elites, these beliefs had permeated the educated classes. Once potential unity was severed, social cleavages were exposed; and these literate commoners embraced progressive notions to a far greater extent than the nobles. Later the deputies of each social stratum would align accordingly in the meeting of the Estates General. Motivating the commoners were pamphlets attacking the Parlements and to some extent the social and religious elite. The example of the American Revolution, which had inspired the French in the 1770s and 1780s, inspired action anew. Critiques of Bourbon "despotism" in previous decades now resonated more. The lampooning of the Church by Voltaire and Diderot and then Montesquieu's widely read *The Spirit of the Laws* which opposed royal overreach and advocated a devolution of power now might seem practical. Also circulating was Rousseau's *Social Contract*, which described a utopia for a small homogenous state. Further, it imagined an egalitarian society in which government almost disappeared, as virtuous citizens with shared values cooperated harmoniously. The most conspicuous among the current works was Abbé Sieyès's *What Is the Third Estate?* (1788), in which he answered his own question, by saying, "Everything." He added that although the Third Estate had been "nothing," it had the right to become "something." Threateningly he also stated that the Third Estate needed to constitute the nation. And more ominously, he noted that if the privileged classes were abolished, the nation in general would be stronger and more prosperous. These powerful claims reflected more than a mere rebalancing of politics, as in country ideology, to include the equality forwarded by notions about natural law and other rights for citizens. In response, Louis XVI doubled the representation of the Third Estate as elections went forward but did not say whether the vote in the Estates General would be by head (which favored the Third Estate) or by estate, as had been by tradition. By the spring, a potential nation, organized around resistance to royal and traditional authorities and established by national rights, was ready to spring.

The French revolutionary decade, 1789

When the Estates General met in Versailles on May 3, nothing had been resolved, but shortly a large step down the revolutionary road occurred. At first, the king indicated the maintenance of the status quo by ordering each Estate to meet separately to verify the credentials of its members. Realizing that acting as an Estate would likely end the possibility of change, the Third Estate declined to take action. Finally on June 17, the Third Estate acted, renaming itself the National Assembly, and in effect claiming alone to represent the nation. On June 20, the delegates arrived at their meeting hall to find it locked. Reassembling at the king's indoor tennis court, the delegates swore to stand together. Three days later, Louis accepted the new political reality and recognized the body as the national assembly. Although many delegates, especially from the clergy, had already joined with the Third Estate, the king ordered the rest to do so.

With many uncertainties everywhere, clearly the king had left in place a representative parliament that stood for the nation. Despite some violence in the countryside, France had moved peacefully toward a version of shared government, perhaps like the constitutional monarchy in Great Britain, but based on a much more populist version of sovereignty. Of course, more radical as well as traditional ideas were oscillating throughout the country, but for the moment a revolution of moderate proportions had been attained. But would this moderation endure? The answer was no, as from these first developments enormous change emerged. Within a few months, a new political and social horizon was created.

Beyond the will of the Assembly lay other pressures that encouraged this great leap into the unknown. Electing the Estates General ended up politicizing the country. Traditionally, although the number of delegates did not at all correspond to the size of the estate being represented, the actual delegates were elected. In this process, voters constructed a list of complaints, called *cahiers*. As the Estates General had not met since 1614, this was the first time in living memory that the public—including workers and peasants—had been polled in this way. The process—in a world with improved communications—increased the size of the informed population and doubtless encouraged its involvement. Furthermore, a poor harvest and high prices encouraged complaint and concern, especially by those at the bottom of the economic ladder. In sum, the active interest of the populace demanded a response from the delegates.

But an expectant people and the injection of the American example cannot explain the entirety of events. Here potent social grievances, expressed in the *cahiers*, manifested themselves in iconic events, the fall of the Bastille and the Great Fear. The Paris riots of July 12–14 and the brutal street executions of certain officials did more than warn the king: He must recognize the right of the National Assembly to govern. In part connected to the uprising in Paris, peasants became fearful that aristocrats would loose "brigands" on the countryside and punish them for supporting the revolution. They preempted such by attacking chateaux, carefully burning archives they feared could be used to resurrect "feudalism." The August 4 decrees, in which nobles collaborated in the National Assembly by renouncing their traditional privileges, undoubtedly were a response to this peasant assault. In fact, many aristocratic delegates took the lead in sacrificing their own rights in what has often been termed the "magic" of that night.

The first marker of change occurred with the decrees of August 4, 1789. To appreciate them fully, one must realize that Old Regime France still functioned with the remnants of what some contemporaries called feudalism. Serfdom had been all but abandoned, and in reality in daily life, France seemed a mainly multiclass society with wealth a very large factor. Nonetheless, legally recognized privileges were omnipresent. Nobles did not pay certain taxes, and they had specific monopolies on hunting, keeping doves, and the like. Peasants made vestigial payments to the lord of the manor, and guilds as well as towns and regions still held many monopolies. Office holders generally owned and exploited their positions. In fact, an official position was conferred as a privilege.

But on August 4, this country of people, still subjects of the king, saw most of these privileges disappear as they edged toward equal citizenship. Specifically, all remaining "feudal" rights were eliminated. Although this and subsequent assemblies would spend much time defining this new society, the decrees specifically wiped out tax advantages and opened hunting to all. Seigneurial justice and obligations likewise ended. Offices could no longer be sold, and justice was to be free. The Church lost the required tithes which had supported it, and within days the Assembly began to discuss that the state was to begin paying the clergy. Essentially, the France of subjects saw that framework of paternalism and privilege give way to a state that administered a society, whose population now were all equal citizens. In addition, the public—even peasants and some women—had been given a voice to complain, which they did.

What would that state be? The National Assembly, while writing the constitution, turned first to a statement of principles. The "Declaration of the Rights of Man and Citizen" was also designed to align delegates with the nation, preserving them from the anger that had erupted in the countryside. Further, the luster of associating themselves with an American approach could provide additional protection from the actions of the peasantry and urban crowd. Some delegates wanted to issue the principles along with the constitution, but instead the ideas were enacted separately a little over two weeks later, on August 26, 1789, as the Declaration of Rights of Man and Citizen. As historian Marcel Gauchet has pointed out, these principles were in tension because they responded to two goals: the establishment of human rights and the creation of a basis on which a government would be founded.[6]

Contemporaries and later scholars have mainly focused on human rights as the Declaration of the Rights of Man and Citizen endorsed the "natural inalienable, and sacred rights of man." And titled and presented as it was, this document was meant to be a statement of universal rights that would shape future constitutions. Rights thus included equality, liberty, property, and security. Even the right to resistance to oppression would be guaranteed; in fact the document promised the right to revolution. In addition, all distinctions would be based on virtue and talent, not on birth or station as in the past. Further, the preamble averred that the purpose of the Declaration was to "redound to the happiness of all." This document linked personal satisfaction to liberty and equality.

Some articles set limits, noting that liberties would be restrained if they infringed on the liberties of others. Indeed, the Declaration also stated that laws enacted should respond to the general will, which without precise definition, the revolutionary generation as opposed to posterity would have taken as a promise that laws would harmonize with society and not be dictatorial. But the Declaration, in the tradition of country ideology, set the law as the anchor to all of these rights. To be sure, the laws (a word used in the Declaration twelve times) were described as emanating from the nation's sovereignty which the "people" or their "representatives" exercised. Intended was that citizens would control their representatives. Representatives could be held accountable, especially in the regulation of taxation. But different than these "historic" limits, the law could control the rights of individuals. Rights to the free exercise of religion and a free press were guaranteed, as long as order was maintained, and the law would decide when such was the case. In general, law guaranteed justice. The clearest commitment to controlling and elevating the government above the individual, and a clear contradiction to the right of resistance can be seen in the stipulation that "any citizen summoned or seized by virtue of the law must obey instantly; he renders himself culpable by resisting." So much for any right to rebel.

Even though strictures in the Declaration contradicted its emphasis on rights and popular supervision, contemporaries heard the references to these advantages most clearly. The title focused on rights and the preamble made rights the center around which the institutions would pivot. Along with the August Decrees, the Declaration abandoned the Old Regime, replacing it with a society of individuals who had natural rights and deserved responsive government. Thus the strictures of the "Law" notwithstanding, its rights then prevailed. Like the Americans, the French did not see a conflict between historic rights and natural law.

But why were two conflicting notions of rights and limits embedded? First, the right of equality and political control by the public relate to the two traditions of "country" ideology and enlightenment natural law in which goals were enunciated. Why allow such an uncharitable article that guaranteed religion—as long as no one was offended. Here, one must turn to an explanation beyond that of Gauchet. In fact, the document reflected the dreams of its most revolutionary minded delegates who optimistically wanted to enable the revolutionaries. But the document also addressed nightmares and the plots of aristocrats. Thus, the vision of law applied expansively to the virtuous people and negatively to the nefarious.

Another explanation for the emphases on both restrictions and personal liberties resides in the continued power of the language of country and that of human rights. The latter, of course, explains the extraordinary freedom and equality in the Declaration. Further, the focus on law and its role relates to the delegates' view of the future which envisioned a balance of powers that would in fact limit the government while protecting the citizenry. As noted in the American case, laws anchored in custom were also able to hold back interpretations of natural rights that contemporaries found conflicted with tradition. Further, conservatives—those who wished to see the Declaration include duties as well as rights—may have strongly supported the emphasis on law and the restraints promised. Even though a significant focus of these laws was rights oriented, they still held out the theoretical prospect of order. Thus was birthed a document that could serve a wide variety of needs in an Assembly that needed to produce a manifesto in a hurried and difficult situation. The Declaration's symbolic endurance internationally over the last centuries reveals its appeal by serving many agendas.

In the summer of 1789, a new journal, the *Révolutions de Paris*, began to write a history that labeled these events a revolution with no backward looks—the overturn of the past and the embrace of something new. Furthermore, by 1789 through successful and preeminent revolutions, the Americans and the French had linked, somewhat imperfectly, the goals of political equality, personal freedom, and liberty to the practice of revolution. Through the abolition of the crown in August of 1792, the revolutionaries added republicanism to their list of innovations. Soon, however, others modified or even tarnished this definition of republican revolution through further action in the revolutionary decade.

Look up the U.S. Declaration of Rights and the French Declaration of Rights of Man and Citizen. How are they similar? Different?

The revolutionary experiment

The French Revolution evolved its experiment in the next decades with innumerable iterations, lasting at least until the seizure of power by Napoleon in the early 1800s and, for many, into his reign that lasted until 1815. This chapter cannot pursue this trajectory systematically and instead follows the fate of the two discourses that powerfully framed the revolution. First, we shall see how "country" theory evolved and collapsed and likewise how the Enlightenment impulse—particularly its focus on equality before the law—changed and failed at its ultimate end. The first case study concentrates on the most radical expression of country ideology and the reaction to it; the second considers how expansive was the definition of equality by considering the efforts of women and people of color in Saint-Domingue.

French historians have overemphasized the period of calm that ensued after the turmoil of the first few months that ended in October 1789, when a crowd rousted the royal family out of Versailles and brought them to Paris, virtually under house arrest. A new struggle soon ensued over the direction of the revolution. The most radical revolutionaries clustered around the Cordelier Club in Paris. Although the Jacobins met nearby, the Cordeliers provided the strongest believers in liberty, defined primarily as popular sovereignty, as a bulwark against oppression. Descendants of the "country" ideology, they had radicalized this prerevolutionary viewpoint far beyond a balanced polity to one that would turn against monarchy, attack the aristocracy, and regard public officials as objects for intense scrutiny. Although this group provided much of the Jacobin leadership that later presided over the Terror, many proved to be dissenters and during the Terror, disputed the leadership and ended up on the guillotine. From 1789 to 1791, Georges Danton led the Cordeliers which included Marat. Their hero was Robespierre, then a National Assemblyman, who later became their enemy.

The Cordeliers believed, first and foremost, in the political program of direct democracy—powered in part by the notion that all—working men anyway—were created equal. This contrasted to the revolutionary mainstream as it moved forward after 1789 with property restrictions on voting and even larger requirements for candidates for office. In fact, Abbé Sieyès, who earlier had so eloquently argued for equality, contended that representation, an unfortunate necessity, could be justified on the basis, not of birth, but of the differences in the talent of individuals. The Cordeliers would hear none of this, wanting all men to participate. In addition, the revolutionary leadership proposed a king, who with a veto could postpone legislation for a very long period. They constructed a constitutional monarch with some legislative power even as his overall pre-1789 position was highly diminished. Radical opinion found that this Constitution gave far too much power to the king, although from their wariness of all politicians, they did not scorn Louis XVI as much as some other factions did.

To support this viewpoint, the radicals developed their vision of the world and the politics that should prosper in it. They began with a Manichean view of the French in which on one side stood the *peuple* whom they defined as those working with their hands, including day laborers as well as shopkeepers. The Cordeliers believed the *peuple* to be special because they were moral, uncorrupted by the temptations of wealth. Arbitrary legal and social distinctions ought to be abolished; *fraternité* would replace the old hierarchies. Suspicious of the wealthy, the Cordeliers advocated some leveling of incomes. The Cordeliers also viewed the *peuple* as virtuous because they avoided vices that they associated with aristocracy including gambling and sexual depravity. The *peuple* were dedicated to the family, and as further discussed below, a traditional family in which women, satisfied to remain within the home, lived secure in the love of their husbands and children.

Just as important as virtue was knowledge. No longer ignorant, the *peuple* had learned from the teaching of the philosophes. Louis-Marie Prudhomme opined in his *Révolutions de Paris* (October 23, 1790):

> From the moment that the *peuple* opened their eyes at the first glimmer of liberty, nothing has deceived them; the names, the titles, all the social considerations, which formerly held them in a stupid respect, have ceased to impose anything on them; they no longer believe in talismans. This *peuple* is not at all a ferocious beast, which as soon as it felt itself unleashed, threw itself on its enemies; it is rather a *peuple* which, after a long denial of justice, first manifested an only too just impatience and today reasons all its actions.[7]

Thus, according to the Cordeliers, the *peuple*, enlightened, virtuous, and egalitarian (except for women), lived the ideals of the revolution and provided the core of its support.

Arrayed against the *peuple* were their antithesis, the *aristocratie*, in which the Cordeliers included not only the nobility but also the rich, high government officials, and the brigands, poor renegades corrupted by the aristocrats to attack the revolution. The vicious values of egotism, luxury, and vice motivated all these enemies, who with their wealth, could buy political power. Furthermore, because of human weakness, these counterrevolutionaries could spread their rotten values to others. Interestingly, the Cordeliers portrayed this "bad" human nature as more natural than the goodness of the people. The Cordeliers believed that immoral aristocrats could replace moral goals through their diabolical plots to overthrow the revolution. The revolutionaries feared that counterrevolution might triumph through both civil war and foreign invasion.

Delineating a world that consisted of the good people and the evil *aristocratie*, the Cordeliers prescribed popular sovereignty and direct democracy as the formula to preserve the revolution. Everyone should participate in the formal political process. Beyond this political participation a constant vigilance would be necessary. The Cordeliers advocated public denunciations and praised the sacking of the mansion of an aristocrat. Camille Desmoulins, who admired the free speech of the *peuple*, urged shouting down enemies or circulating petitions of denunciation and believed that boycotts against antirevolutionary plays might work.

The radicals advocated violence. The assault on the Bastille was an iconic event worthy of emulation. In reaction to the notion that impoverished debtors should be imprisoned, one journalist wrote "blood must flow," if necessary to keep such men free.[8] In all the revolution, no one more forcefully advocated violence than the Cordeliers' Jean-Paul Marat, who already in 1790 was urging that 20,000 be sacrificed to preserve the revolution. Furthermore, he named individuals, including Lafayette, who ought to be executed.

The radicals' goals went beyond surveillance and repression to include making the institutions of government as weak as possible. The people should have the capacity to recall deputies, individually or collectively, at any time; and legislative deliberations should always be open to the public. Likewise, jurists should have limited authority and should follow strict procedures regarding arrests and trials. Juries should rule in civil as well as criminal cases. If necessary, the courtroom spectators could object and negate the power of the judge. And, of course, the executive, if the office existed at all, must be exceptionally weak, and formal restrictions should limit his authority. Marat wanted to limit the king's oversight to foreign policy and command of the troops on the frontier. Moreover, the Cordeliers held that no standing army should exist, as such forces might be hostile to the revolution.

The radical political philosophy enunciated by the Cordeliers, at first with almost no support in the National Assembly, gradually gained adherents in Paris and nationally. Eventually, as the Jacobin Club repeatedly divided, lost members, and further radicalized, important elements of this vision of politics increasingly became theirs. To some extent, this outlook even enabled their rising popularity, at least in Paris, as early as the autumn of 1791. Nonetheless, once in power these same Jacobins could not tolerate direct democracy opposing their efforts. Internecine warfare broke out between those who remained Cordeliers and claimed to represent the *peuple* and the rest; this division led directly to suppression of the Cordeliers and the end of the experiment with radical democracy. In the end, the revolutionary idea would not mean direct democratic action.

To understand this turn of events requires some chronology. Although collaborating with the Cordeliers had helped them push out more moderate leadership and assume power in the summer of 1793, the Jacobins found themselves in charge of a government under siege from civil war, attack from monarchical powers, and continued agitation from the Paris street including the Cordeliers. To counter these problems and defend the revolution as they envisioned it, the Jacobins, led by Robespierre, began in the late summer to create the most autocratic regime of the revolutionary decade, including a political Terror aimed at enemies and threats. Even before seizing power, having already been the force behind the execution of Louis XVI, they added Marie-Antoinette to the victims. Furthermore, these Jacobins in seeking to discipline the country executed "enemies" real and imagined and brooked no opposition. Doubtless, the war with foreign monarchs and the counterrevolution in the provinces did more to stimulate authoritarian rule, but the Cordeliers were also a problem and suffered for their actions. Their impertinence could not be tolerated and the leadership went to the guillotine. In addition, Robespierre and allies instituted a reign of Terror that also could not designate fairly its enemies. When the government fell in July 1794, even though their centralized, disciplined, and repressive policies had turned the war to France's advantage, they were not lamented. Nonetheless, they had pioneered a potent dictatorship for revolutionary survival and victory, even though they also overturned democratic revolutionary goals. To some extent, they did compensate the working classes through policies if not participation. The Jacobins, unwilling to abandon private property, aided laborers by, among other programs, supporting education, permitting divorce (which helped women abandoned by their husbands), and scouring the countryside for foodstuffs. Their drive, programs, and focus later impressed Marx and others who conceived of a dictatorship of the proletariat as a bridge to a socialist society.

After the fall of the Jacobins, the French reverted to a carefully managed representative democracy for the next five years. With the monarchy finished, the monarchical concept at least temporarily discredited, and property qualifications designed to deny most laborers the vote, a shaky republic governed. Former Jacobins, moderates like those of 1789, and royalists competed for power. Buffeted by the disconsolate—both those who wanted more and those who wanted less revolution—the leaders of this so-called Directory engineered a series of coups.

One of these governmental overthrows led to the one-man government of Napoleon Bonaparte replacing the ineffectual republic in 1799. Launching his regime as a three-person consulate, Napoleon soon created an empire and gave himself the role of "Emperor for life." Bonaparte was perhaps the most innovative political actor of the entire period. Despite having upended democracy, undermined liberty, and increasingly acted as a dictator, he clothed all of this in revolutionary rhetoric. A new legislature was created—under his heavy-handed control. Although he made peace with the Pope, he snubbed the Church by crowning himself emperor, denying the Church the right of granting sacrality to his self-appointed imperial royal power. Religion and revolutionary secularism could coexist. Bonaparte permitted the expatriate nobles back into the country, but also allowed those who purchased confiscated church and noble land during the revolution to retain it. Above all, Napoleon defined himself as a man of the people as he personally led his troops into battle and exposed himself to great danger. He claimed to embody the revolutionary ideas, even as he subverted the revolutionary principles of individual rights, free speech, and a free press. Beyond this cynical accumulation of political power, he gained popularity by enacting important programs in education, the separation of Church and state, political rights for some minorities, and making available social progress for the poor as well as some assistance for women. All these ambiguities allowed him more actual power than eighteenth-century French monarchs had exercised as well as the celebrity of popular support. Others, even Communists such as Fidel Castro and Mao Zedong and many dictators in Latin American and elsewhere, later repeated Napoleon's approach. Only his overreach in attacking Moscow and defeat by the allies eventually cost him his imperial throne in 1815.

Having previously adopted the most extreme versions of equality and liberty, the Cordeliers perished. Replacing them were a later generation of liberal revolutionaries (who took power in 1830) and then others with revolutionary ideas who later tried to extend this experiment of direct democracy and meaningful elections into new republics in 1848 and 1870.

The search for equality for women and slaves

Based in part on Enlightenment notions of natural law and equality, the French Revolution inspired a desire for women to be treated fairly with men, but in fact it seemed that feminism and sexism rose in tandem. The Declaration of the Rights of Women, written by Olympe de Gouges in 1791, was possibly the most visible and notable articulation of women's goals. Paralleling the Declaration of Rights of Man, it shows how one prominent revolutionary specifically spoke out for women. Like its predecessor, the document consisted of a preamble and seventeen articles and followed the same structure. In fact, the articles often simply demanded that all rights apply to women as well.

Beyond seeking equality with men, this document focused on the realities for women. The articles analyzed women's condition and its possible improvement. Curiously, its assertions agree with some of the most sexist beliefs regarding court women in the Old Regime. In fact, de Gouges concurred with Rousseau and others that essential to the success of aristocratic women at Versailles had been their reliance on "ruse" and "dissimulation." And in this view, the government relied on the "nocturnal administration" of such shameless women to ensnare and control "men, profane and sacred." But, in considering the circumstances of unmarried women deserted by their lovers, De Gouges proposed that revolutionaries offer a solution for women attached to wealthy men: equally divide community property. Unfortunately, for the poor, in most cases, only poverty and "opprobrium" were possible. And de Gouges concluded her analysis, calling upon male legislators to remedy the extraordinary vulnerability of unmarried mothers who could lodge no claims against the fathers of their children.

For the married, De Gouges proposed a contract to protect the financial interests of women and their children. She also argued:

> I offer a foolproof way to elevate the soul of women; it is to join them to all the activities of man; if man persists in finding this way impractical, let him share his fortune with women, not at his caprice, but by the wisdom of laws. Prejudice falls, morals are purified, and nature regains all her rights.

She closed her plans with somewhat a non-sequitur, a defense of the recent legislation which gave free men of color equal rights with whites. Her advanced thinking condemned those who defied natural rights of equality, by discriminating on the basis of the "scantiest tint" of their blood. And she concluded: "A divine hand serves to spread liberty throughout the realms of man ...."

Obviously, despite de Gouges's complaint that the Old Regime and even the revolution gave few chances to women, she could speak out and even imagine an egalitarian society (though she was executed in 1793, possibly for her feminism but also for her anti-Jacobin political views and associations). New expectations and openings did come to exist for educated women along with advantages for women more generally. In the disorders that broke out, women participated, notably in the uprising in October 1789 when a mass march, led by women, brought Louis XVI and his family from Versailles to Paris. The famous Old Regime intellectual Condorcet, when later a revolutionary, wrote in 1790 fully in support of women's political rights. Although these rights were not achieved, and in fact French women did not receive the vote until 1944, the revolution provided improvements in social and economic matters. Most prominent was the legalization of divorce in the revolution (though again illegal from 1816 to 1884), which as noted above was especially important to women because marital breakdown usually left them with children yet without legal recourse against their husbands.

Other substantial benefits were provided for women. During the era of Jacobin leadership of 1793–1794, that government legislated favorably, as de Gouges had wished, in regard to support from putative fathers and siblings sharing parental property. Other efforts included allowing illegitimate children to inherit. Ironically, as Olwen Hufton has pointed out, counterrevolutionary women also saw other types of benefits as the reaction against the revolution pushed the Church to provide necessary charity for vulnerable women in local parishes. In a sense, the revolutionary divide created fissures where women could find social assistance as well as participate actively in the political process.

In spite of these opportunities, women faced an enormous sexism, present from the Enlightenment but energized anew in the revolution. As mentioned previously, some philosophes, believing women in the public sphere to be wicked, asserted that they used lies and sexual favors to gain power at court. Salons run by women also revealed, to Rousseau in particular, that women were promoting luxury instead of the sturdy virtues. And no one wrote more powerfully that women should remain in the home than did Jean-Jacques in his prerevolutionary *Emile* (1762).

Revolutionary women had to contend with this same sexism, heightened by the scapegoating of Marie-Antoinette. Already under attack in the Old Regime, she became the target of vitriolic assaults after 1789. According to her detractors, she was an important source of treachery through her participation in the Austrian Committee, designed to overthrow the revolution. Just to make her involvement clear, journalists labeled this group the "comité austrichienne." Although the masculine noun comité should have been followed by a masculine adjective, the feminine form of Austrian was used—clearly referring to Austrian-born Marie-Antoinette and her purported treason. Pornographers went even further and graphically portrayed the Queen in bed with women and with the king's brother. Even as she stood at the social apogee for women in the realm, she received brutal treatment. At her trial for treason in 1793, the prosecutor accused her of sexually molesting her own son. Marie-Antoinette was not alone in receiving such attacks. For example, Olympe de Gouges, for her political involvement, was guillotined as an "unnatural woman." Indeed, the new female political clubs were also silenced during the Terror, in part because they challenged the regime. Other groups were repressed, yet this treatment also seems to show a special animus toward female assertiveness.

In short, the revolution offered a theoretical potential to address women's issues (as de Gouges asserted), and many sought to use this cataclysmic event as an opportunity for advancing the rights of women. But sexist rhetoric competed with actual improvements and denied feminist viewpoints. Although Napoleon also proved to be a reactionary in this area, the struggle went on to become one of the legacies of the revolutionary idea of human rights—as Mary Wollstonecraft also asserted in England. However, no political revolution during or since the eighteenth century seems to have been fully invested in the equality of women. Although women repeatedly joined revolutions, their own cause did not greatly advance through this form of change. Possibly the combination of revolutionary openings and sexist rhetoric produced contradictory ends with some deterred and others motivated to advance female equality.

Another area in which the revolution's emphasis on equality had a direct but limited impact was slavery. Surprisingly enough, during the Revolution's most radical phase, the French revolutionaries eliminated this institution throughout France's colonies in 1794.

In fact, as the belief in human rights evolved in the eighteenth century, slavery had come under increased scrutiny. In Philadelphia in 1775 and then in France in 1788, proposals circulated to ameliorate the lot of slaves, and there were even attempts to abolish it altogether. However, in both the American and French revolutions, the commitment to life, liberty, and other rights for all humanity usually did not include slaves. The U.S. Constitution of 1789 left the status of bondsmen and bondswomen to the individual states. In fact, insofar as the document referred to slaves, it used the phrase "those bound to service" who, for purposes of representation and taxation, were to be counted as three-fifths of a person. The French Constitution of 1791 was more direct: it reaffirmed the legality of slavery. Both countries saw this as a matter of maintaining very valuable slave economies and indeed racializing the concept of slavery to exclude "whites."

While abolition in America had some supporters but little change in this era, matters in France evolved from a very unpromising start rather suddenly after 1791. Although the French held a number of colonies in the New World and around the Indian Ocean, Saint-Domingue (increasingly called Haiti during the revolution) was the most important colony and one of the richest places in the world. In fact, after the defeat in the Seven Years War, when the French had to decide whether to retain either Canada or Saint-Domingue, they chose the latter for its economic power. Built on coffee and sugar cultivation, Saint-Domingue in 1789 included 500,000 slaves, 28,000 free people of color (black and mulatto), and 32,000 whites. At the establishment of the National Assembly, whites in Saint-Domingue immediately wanted to participate and sent representatives, apparently not considering that the principle of representation might include others (or perhaps fearing that it *might* be applied to others). Not surprisingly, members of the National Assembly, some of whom had been sympathetic to those of African descent before the revolution, began to urge rights for free men of color. While these delegates did not consider including women or the enslaved, this new push would have made all free men citizens. Journalists, activists, and, as we have seen, Olympe de Gouges sought to go further, abolishing slavery altogether. But the National Assembly, sensitive to the potential reaction of the whites on the island and the possibility of revolt, as well as the economic consequences, was not willing to do so.

Retaining the slave regime became increasingly difficult, but the French legislature tried, passing a law on March 30, 1790, exempting Saint-Domingue from any movement toward legal equality. But free people of color were not deterred, and an armed rebellion of free blacks occurred in the fall of 1790. The French army, aided by local planter militias, ruthlessly put down the rebels, executing many, including the leader, James Ogé. After renewed agitation, the National Assembly granted free men of color voting rights if both of the man's parents had been free. But white resistance kept the colony on edge.

Revolutionary contagion spread, however; and on August 22, 1791, the slaves of Saint-Domingue rose in rebellion. This explosion, fueled by terrible conditions and the optimism of revolution, continued over the next several years. No matter what the National Assembly tried to do, stanching the fervor of the slaves was difficult, if not impossible. Surely the tropical conditions, which felled many French soldiers through disease, contributed to French incapacity. Also, in the age of sail, the supply line from France was long. Finally, the French were hardly the only imperial power in the Caribbean, and the Spanish (who occupied the other half of the island with Saint-Domingue) and the British with their colonies in the region welcomed the opportunity to enhance their own power or at least diminish that of the French.

But if it is evident in retrospect that the slaves, more numerous and more motivated than their opponents, would eventually gain freedom, abolition actually came somewhat haltingly. In fact, the legislature had first responded to demands for racial equality by hardening its stance and stripping the recently conferred rights of citizenship from the free men of color. Angered by this measure, the slaves violently defeated intransigent planters.

Months later, the legislature reversed itself and in the fall of 1792 sent two representatives (Sonthonax and Polverel), whose goal was to quell violence between the whites and the free people of color by healing the rift. In fact, the situation spilled out of control, because as the commissioners treated the non-whites equally, the formerly privileged whites reacted negatively. To the slaves, the commissioners reemphasized the Code Noir, drawn up by Louis XIV in 1685, which restricted the most punitive measures of the planters but did not point toward freedom. Thus the slave insurrection continued.

A stalemate ensued until May 1793, when the French general Galbaud arrived to take command of the military forces in Saint-Domingue. Jeremy Popkin, in his superb book on the revolution in

Saint-Domingue, has chronicled how Galbaud's arrival unhinged this very dangerous situation.[9] Complex issues separated the general, commissioners, and local forces; and this combustible situation erupted on July 19, when Galbaud authorized and led an assault on the town of Cap-François, supported by the navy in the town's harbor, to regain control for the whites. This battle's outcome hung in doubt until the commissioners, who to save Saint-Domingue for France had by then aligned themselves with the armed slave forces, persuaded the latter to join the fray. How did they do this? On June 21, commissioners Sonthonax and Polverel offered freedom to all those joining them. Before the threat and fear of the "savages" as Galbaud's forces imagined their black opponents, the whites crumbled. Having been saved by armed slaves who responded to the offer of freedom, the commissioners, to stabilize their authority and that of France, had no choice but to extend the offer of freedom to all slaves. This was the only assurance that could work.

Thus, because of an impulsive act by Galbaud and a desperate response by Sonthonax and Polverel, slavery ended locally and then throughout Saint-Domingue. This approach took a while to become firm. By April 1794, Toussaint L'Ouverture, the most famous leader of the slaves, had allied his troops with the other slaves. All that was then necessary was confirmation of this emancipation from the government in Paris. But this too was no guaranteed matter. In fact, the white settlers who fled Saint-Domingue had settled in the United States and deployed ambassadors to plead their cause in Paris. With the chain of events still not known in Paris, the destruction of Cap-François seemed in itself proof of the failure of Sonthonax and Polverel. Further, the commissioners were politically linked to Brissot whom Robespierre had pushed from power and had executed as a traitor. Moreover, Robespierre, who had once denounced slavery, had come to support it, perhaps because as he now felt responsible for France's economic welfare, the principle of abolition seemed less important. The commissioners almost alone had to push the case for abolition. To justify their own actions, and likely from personal convictions, they urged the point. Although Jeremy Popkin carefully details the debate in the legislature and among the revolutionary leadership, he too was unable to determine exactly how the commissioners prevailed; a general emancipation, in short, was in no way preordained. On February 14, 1794, however, the revolutionary convention voted rather abruptly to abolish slavery, not only in Saint-Domingue but throughout French dominions.

In sum, rebellious slaves and an unexpected political process both in Saint-Domingue and Paris led to the principles of the Declaration of Rights of Man and Citizen being applied to the institution of slavery. As noted, this earthquake in human relations and rights, while hardly inevitable, was immense. It also added a new element to the idea of revolution by extending the rights of man to formerly enslaved Africans in all of France's colonies.

In a postscript, the French later tried once again to re-enslave the island. In 1802, Napoleon, then in power, sent an army to re-establish slavery and French control in Saint-Domingue. Losses from diseases and from the military actions of the ex-slaves led to the French withdrawal and eventually to recognition of the new nation's independence (in 1825). Haiti became the first modern nation in 1804 to definitively abolish slavery. Slaves alone made sure there was no reversion to enslavement in that period. Meanwhile, the French managed to reestablish the slave system in other French colonies, including Guadeloupe and Martinique. Slavery would not be finally abolished in French colonies until the later Revolution of 1848. Meanwhile, many Latin American nations, beginning with Mexico, had ended slavery soon after gaining independence from Spain. Slavery would also be widely abolished during the next eighty years, though revolution would not always be necessary. The United States prohibited slavery only after an extremely violent Civil War—which was in some respects the final phase of the American Revolution.

The democratic revolutions of the United States and France overthrew governments and created societies based in principle on human and customary rights. Although the revolutionaries claimed the rights for all humanity, educated white men made extravagant claims and when tested, proved that they mainly meant for themselves. But others—especially women and slaves—sought eagerly to expand their own claims. Somewhat surprisingly from an historic retrospective, in which racism has proven more virulent and durable than sexism, at the time of the revolution black slaves advanced their rights more than women. Further, the French Revolution also created an enhanced desire for wide political participation. And if direct democracy and surveillance never emerged and, as Rousseau and Montesquieu hoped, it has advanced. After all, even Napoleon nominally allowed voting and a legislature.

In sum, though the utopian goals predictably failed, the revolution opened the door that many would walk through in the next two centuries. For those who supported the revolution, the disappointments, deaths, and sacrifices did not go unredeemed. And in fact, as subsequent chapters will show, the French and the American revolutions clearly pioneered a political technique that was malleable, expandable, and deployed very frequently to propagate the agenda for social, economic, and political change.

Consider the modern political world. How are the different types of rights—country or natural—used by different political parties?

Essay 1

Edmund Burke, *Reflections on the Revolution in France* (1790) and Thomas Paine, *The Rights of Man* (1790)

Writing in response to the nonconformist minister Richard Price's laudatory support for the French Revolution, Edmund Burke found his essay provoked a rejoinder from Thomas Paine. These two extended pamphlets provided lengthy, rather unorganized visions of the French Revolution. Well circulated at the time and enjoying an audience into the present, Burke's long essay has been seen as the iconic conservative critique of revolution while Paine's was an enthusiastic response favoring the revolution, undampened by its tempestuous troughs and failures. Commentators have considered Burke and Paine as the founders of two opposing streams of thought.

Here I propose through an analysis of these two discourses to provide a deeper understanding of the revolution and its detractors. Although not typical, exemplary, or average, Burke and Paine, who were passionately interested in the revolution, allow a more complex understanding of the revolutionary experience. Their justifications and criticisms give clues to the mainspring of their views. What were they defending or attacking; what mattered; and thus, why leap into the fight? Millions of people in Europe, whether they experienced the revolution closely or afar, had to decide what they thought and even what they would do.

Edmund Burke wrote his famous attack before difficulties started to pile up for the revolution in France in 1791. His note, so discordant, might suggest to later generations how prescient was the English sage, but his peers found instead that it was easier to think how precipitant and churlish it was to attack a new system at its very beginning. Because Burke had supported the American Revolution, contemporaries hardly expected his diatribe in 1789. However, while his view toward the American colonies was based on parliamentary politics and in-fighting, Burke's interpretation in 1789 was more philosophical.

And attack Burke did: the essay in form appears a sledgehammer hitting again and again. Although the attacks somewhat differed, they reinforce one another. While this repetition may try a modern reader's patience, yet it made its points eminently understandable. Such a long essay also must have challenged readers by raising some doubt about whether Burke, in his return to similar themes over and again, was adding to his argument or simply adding to his list of revolutionary failures.

Burke organized his attack on the French Revolution by explaining the proper principle of government as exemplified by the English government, then condensing the concepts underlying the revolution, and finally relating how these revolutionary principles destroyed a previously capable French society and government.

The fixed pole underlying Burke's viewpoint was the naturalness of the traditional. A system that emerged from long experience was far better fitted to humans than an abstraction such as human rights. In fact, Burke laid out his view historically from the Magna Carta (1215) to the Declaration of Rights (1688). "Our liberties come as an inheritance: ... the people of England well know, that the idea of inheritance furnishes a sure principle of conservatism, and a sure principle of transmission ...." And he waxed: "The institution of policy, the goals of fortune, the gifts of Providence, are handed down to us and from us, in the same course and order. Our political system is placed in a just correspondence and symmetry with the order of the world ...."[10] By passing rights on through generations, Burke argued that family relations guaranteed "fundamental laws." This linkage of law with human institutions suggested that stability and change were in fact organic, not theoretical. Interestingly, Burke asserted that governments must allow for change or they will fail, but change should be little as will accomplish the job. And to show the genius of the English system, he repeatedly pointed to the Revolution of 1688, which was fondly remembered as a peaceable change and labeled as the "Glorious Revolution" because in fact it was no revolution but a coup, or a circulation of elites. Burke, however, remained silent regarding the takeover of power by Cromwell in the 1650s, a radical development that did not fit with his view of English history. More "French Revolution" than "Glorious," the earlier English Revolution was a violent transfer of power. Burke likely excised it because it ran counter to his point about the seamless tradition of England.

Corollary to Burke's view of history and tradition were his opinions on the proper use of liberty, the role of ability and property, and the central place of religion. In fact, to Burke liberty was not something to strive for but something that the English already had attained. As the birthright of Englishmen living in a free country, liberty in Burke's view had been secured and only needed to be protected. To arrive at this view, Burke had defined liberty for the average person not as voting but as not being oppressed by government. A long section gave his view that the French, in their struggle for liberty, were in fact destroying it, even devastating the country.

Burke believed that the role of the propertied and religion would secure liberty, and its anchor, tradition. Burke was particularly vociferous in his support for elites: "Nothing is a due and adequate representative of a state that does not represent its ability, as well as its property." In short, while many might award power and authority to merit, Burke would give those to property. Here the reason is simple. He believed that while ability was volatile, property was "sluggish" rather than temperamental. Indeed, those with great property ought to exercise even more weight because they would be immune from too much passion. In summary, property "grafts benevolence upon avarice" and even the organization of the House of Commons gave property its due. In a somewhat apologetic tone, Burke continued: "Let those large proprietors be what they will and they have their chance at being among the best, they are at the very worst, the ballast of the vessel of the commonwealth."[11]

Burke thought that religion also lay at the core of the ship of state. He clearly indicated his devotion to religion and evoked nature to affirm his view: "We know and it is our pride to know, that man is by his constitution a religious animal; and that atheism is against, not only our reason but our instincts ...." Voicing the concern that if France, caught in its "delirium" rejected religion, he expostulated, "what terrible dictators might take its place?"[12] Asserting that religion—in the form of the Anglican Church—resulted from profound wisdom, he argued that its ministers stood for God. Simply their anointment proved God's favor. In fact, for Burke the key institutions in England included church, king, and aristocracy.

Not only was Burke clear about what he held dear, but his acrimony toward the French Revolution was intense and unremitting regarding its principles and actions. He depicted the revolution as the inverse of English institutions. For example, both countries prized liberty, but English liberty, in his view, had less to do with politics than the opportunity to conduct one's private life without governmental interference. Public life should be for only the few. Burke's essay described revolutionary France as a place where all asserted their right to participate. Such liberty seemed to him purely unrestrained and thoroughly objectionable. In a very telling remark, he stated that French liberty destroyed all precedents and exploded all. By substituting "the rights of man," the French revolutionaries averred that "any thing [sic] withheld from their full demand is so much of fraud and injustice."[13] In other words, liberty was license.

Moreover, Burke assailed the workings of the revolution, whose first crime was to attack King Louis XVI. He also defended other parts of the Old Regime, including the nobility who were attacked by jealous individuals. Perhaps, he mused, reform was desirable but certainly not obliteration as "Nobility is a graceful ornament to the civil order. It is the Corinthian capital of political society."[14] In the course of his essay, Burke examined various revolutionary social and economic policies and found them deplorable.

All of these arguments evoked a reaction from Tom Paine, who though born in England had argued the cause of the American colonies in his famous pamphlet, *Common Sense* (1776). In fact, Paine turned each of Burke's arguments on its head by using logic and history. For example, he asserted that hereditary property began when someone first took something from another. Paine believed that the aristocrats rather than being the center of gravity that kept matters on the proper path were in fact authors of theft. And the English king was no more than a German usurper. Moreover, Paine defended the revolutionary principle of liberty and went to great lengths to show the benefits of a democratic system. He rewrote the history of the French Revolution to exonerate it as completely as possible.

For example, consider Burke's and Paine's version of the attack on the Bastille. The English aristocrat not only adhered to his principles but noted the defects of revolution through its violence and other failures. After Burke dwelt on excesses of the revolutions, Paine took him to task for his interpretation of July 14. While allowing that the crowd in the uprising killed some, Paine excused those deaths with the supposition that the crowd had learned this violence from the Old Regime government. Even in England, the people had " ... been accustomed to behold ... the head stuck upon spikes, which remained for years upon the Temple Bury ...." Paine also alluded to the horrific execution in France of Damiens who had attempted to assassinate Louis XV and in retaliation was torn apart by horses. Further, Paine argued that rather than the French people bearing responsibility, it fell to the few who carried out the sentence. But why did this occur? Seeing it as an aspect of the degradation of the people by their government, Paine indicated that the National Assembly and the government of Paris had brought brutality to a halt. "Never were more pains taken to instruct and enlighten mankind, and to make them so that the interest consisted in this virtue, and not in their revenge ...."[15]

Paine and Burke both resorted to history. The antique history of England showed Burke the best way to construct a society; Paine attacked such a view with his interpretation of the recent history of the French, and at times, the new American republic. Yet Paine also believed that this new history did not merely consist of the repeated behaviors called history, but was infused with natural law, its principles embedded in the system. Thus, divine providence had provided a benevolent system within nature itself that the French revolutionaries had mobilized.

Even beyond a different conception of history and a deistic, natural view of God instead of a theistic one, a very profound difference in tone emerged regarding the revolution. An enthusiast, Paine, described a utopia and its brilliance. The conclusion to the first part of the *Rights of Man* (an addendum was published in 1792) revealed his optimism about man in a republic, where he "sees the *rationale* of the whole system, its origins, and its operations; and as it is best supported when best understood, the human faculties act with boldness and acquire, under this form of government, a gigantic manliness."[16] Whether Paine chose his last word by design or instinct, he was writing in the revolutionary period when masculinity was positively gendered and femininity equated with decadence.

Further, he believed that a society with equal representation would command the wholehearted support of the public. Taxes would be accepted as necessary. Paine continued: "what we now see in the world, from the world, from the revolutions of America and France, is a renovation of the natural order of things, a system of principles as unweird as truth and the existence of man, and combining moral and political happiness and natural property."[17] Paine then concluded about the inevitability of the revolution's triumph:

> From what we now see, nothing of reform on the political world ought to be held improbable. It is an age of revolutions, in which every thing may be looked for. The intrigue of courts, by which the system of war is kept up, may provoke a confederation of nations to abolish it; and an European Congress, to patronize the progress of free government, and promote the civilization of nations with each other, is an event nearer in probability, than once were the revolutions and alliance of France and America.[18]

On every issue, Paine and Burke differed. In retrospect it seems easy to see why they chose as they did, although Burke's course mystified some contemporaries. Because he had, in fact, supported the American revolutionaries and even endorsed some of their ideas, the extent of his opposition to the French Revolution shocked the French. Most likely Burke's embrace of the American colonists' cause was related to aristocratic opposition to George III's accumulation of power and Burke's apparent inclination toward the commonwealth man ideology that sought to minimize high-handed authority. By 1789, the issues clearly appeared as revolution against the status quo ante and in favor of natural rights egalitarianism, which a man of his background was hardly likely to endorse. In contrast, Tom Paine's defense of the French Revolution followed logically from earlier views. Emigrating to America after a difficult life in England, he immediately associated himself with the revolutionary tide. His pamphlet *Common Sense* which attacked George III was a sensation and surely rallied the patriots. Back in London by 1787, he found himself inclined to the revolutionary stirrings in France. And once again he intervened by writing a pamphlet *The Rights of Man* to support them.

Not only does the print war of Burke and Paine illuminate the revolution, their rhetorical stance suggests much about the emerging conflict. The two completely antithetical positions that soon emerged anticipated the fierce battle that ensued between counterrevolutionaries and revolutionaries. Indeed, the rhetoric employed gave those economically, psychologically, socially, or philosophically inclined to either side a strong platform of righteousness on which to stand. Even more revealingly, these two positions may help explain why, at least at first, the revolutionaries had the upper hand. In fact, Burke's position bespoke sobriety and a defense of the status quo. Paine, on the other hand, described a secular heaven of endless possibilities. In our rather cynical world, where revolutionary history and realities compete with idealism, the two sides might be differently matched. But in that period, when the Enlightenment and local struggles against monarchy and aristocracy held the upper hand, Paine likely came out on top. And he sold 80,000 copies to Burke's 30,000—but this proves somewhat inconclusive because Paine's cost much less than his rival's.

Some call Burke the first modern conservative. Would modern conservatives agree with him and he with them?

Further Reading

Armitage, David. *The Declaration of Independence: A Global History*. Cambridge, MA, 2007.

Bailyn, Bernard. *The Ideological Origins of the American Revolution*. Cambridge, MA, 1962.

Blanning, T.C.W. *The French Revolutionary Wars, 1787–1802*. London, 1996.

Brown, Howard. *Ending the French Revolution: Violence, Justice, and Repression from the Terror to Napoleon*. Charlottesville, 2006.

Countryman, Edward. *The American Revolution*, 2nd Ed. New York, 2003.

Fitzsimmons, Michael P. *The Night the Old Regime Ended: August 4, 1789 and the French Revolution*. University Park, PA, 2003.

Godineau, Dominique. *The Women of Paris and Their French Revolution*. Berkeley, 1998.

Hammersley, Rachel. *The English Republican Tradition and Eighteenth-Century France: Between the Ancients and the Moderns*. Manchester, 2010.

Hufton, Olwen H. *Women and the Limits of Citizenship in the French Revolution*. Toronto, 1992.

Hunt, Lynn. *Inventing Human Rights: A History*. New York, 2007.

Jasanoff, Maya. *Liberty's Exiles: American Loyalists in a Revolutionary World*. New York, 2011.

Kates, Gary. *The Cercle Social, the Girondins, and the French Revolution*. Princeton, 1985.

Middlekauff, Robert. *The Glorious Cause: The American Revolution, 1763–1789*. New York, 1982.

Polasky, Janet. *Revolutions without Borders: The Call to Liberty in the Atlantic World*. New Haven, 2015.

Sewell, William H., Jr. *A Rhetoric of Bourgeois Revolution: The Abbé Sieyès and What Is the Third Estate?*. Durham and London, 1994.

Tackett, Timothy. *When the King Took Flight*. Cambridge, MA, 2003.

Van Kley, Dale. Ed. *The French Idea of Freedom: The Old Regime and the Declaration of Rights of 1789*. Stanford, 1994.

Wood, Gordon. *The Radicalism of the American Revolution*. New York, 1992.

2

Latin America and Europe and the New National and Economic Meanings of Revolution, 1800–1871

With the idea of revolution established in the "West," and firmly linked to general conceptions of legal equality and democracy, the following chapters examine the way that the concept of revolution mutated and added different beliefs during the next two centuries. To expand this examination from two main locales—the British North American colonies and France—to a worldwide phenomenon necessitates a far more general approach: thus the focus will be more on the ideas than their sources, more on major new accretions than the changes in older ones; revolutionary themes that were most prominent and diasporic will be emphasized. Considering the deployment of ideas in Latin American revolutions, a huge new beachhead from its origins, this chapter then focuses on the two big "isms" that played such a large role in future revolutions: nationalism and socialism. In regard to this first notion, the unification of Italy provides an important example.

Although Marx made no revolution, his successors did, so we must examine the origin of the Marxist ideology. In its essay, to elaborate on these new ideas, the chapter analyzes the differing views of the revolution of 1848 in France between the "liberal" social and political analyst Alexis de Tocqueville and Karl Marx, the most systematic and widely known scholar and activist in the revolutionary tradition. This contrast will deepen the understanding of the revolutionary waves that swept both sides of the Atlantic as well as show the impulses and resistance to change.

Latin America

Beyond France and the United States, revolutions spread globally, beginning with the Latin American revolutions in the early nineteenth century. South of the British colonies, from the middle of North America to the tip of South America, lay lands claimed by Portugal and Spain. The latter's territories began with Mexico and occupied much of the Caribbean and Central and South America, with the large exception of the huge area of Brazil dominated by Portugal. In 1800, all seemed comfortably ruled by Europeans. By 1825, all except a few small territories were independent.

Despite the enormous variety of the Latin American countries in history, landscape, and population mix (consisting of slaves, indigenous peoples, those of mixed race, Europeans [or peninsulars], and creoles [white individuals born in America]), scholars tend to emphasize creole leadership in the revolutions that led to independence. Of course, many others held grievances, not only toward Iberian rule but toward creoles, peninsulars, and colonial administrators. The creoles, as an upper-class elite, took the lead. More important, they were well educated and heavily influenced by the progressive notions that had led to revolution elsewhere.

Events in Europe also significantly contributed to the Latin American drive for independence. Numerous rebellions and uprisings occurred in Latin America from 1500 on, despite growing Spanish efforts at repression from the mid-eighteenth century. Despite urban rebellions in Brazil in the wake of the French Revolution, and the Tupac Amorce II rebellion in the Andes in 1780–1783, these violent events did not seem to lead directly to independence movements. In fact, the most destabilizing factor may have been the sharp decline after 1800 in Spanish and Portuguese power over the lands and peoples under their dominion. The depletion of silver in American mines also hurt the economies of Spain and Portugal. Moreover the French Revolution, especially the Napoleonic invasion and rule of Iberia, accelerated problems. The attenuation of Iberian power in the Americas occurred in several different ways. Let us consider the major areas.

In fact, Brazil achieved independence without a serious violent revolution. Under siege for much of the revolutionary decade of the 1790s, Portugal the following decade moved its court, with the help of the French fleet, to Rio de Janeiro. Despite Napoleon's defeat and retreat from Portugal in 1811, the Portuguese court ruled by Prince John remained in Rio. And in 1815, he declared Brazil a separate kingdom. Eventually, financial difficulties led to a military uprising in Portugal itself; the Portuguese government then declared a constitutional monarchy. Still it was some time before the king was willing to return to Portugal; only after a successful Portuguese liberal revolution in 1821 did he acquiesce. Later that same year the Portuguese government began to demand greater obedience, and the Brazilians rejected such demands. Pedro, the son of John, refused to cave in and accepted the title of the Emperor of Brazil. A short military conflict ensued and resulted in the defeat of Portugal and full independence for the former colony. Although Brazil gained its freedom, politically a powerful emperor ruled along with a parliament elected by a very limited franchise.

Mexico, or New Spain, as it was known, followed another path. Under Spanish rule, this territory extended well into the modern borders of the United States, including the Southwest and California. While serious peasant revolts occurred in Mexico even beyond 1814, these efforts met defeat; only activity by a significant segment of creoles actually changed the political system. What mobilized this class was the action in 1820 by the Spanish Parliament, liberal at home, but repressive abroad, that generated elite opposition. While enacting changes at home, the legislature made manifest its intention of keeping Mexico subservient. Augustine de Iturbide and the mixed-race Vicente Guerrero led the opposition, which first sought a liberal catholic monarchy that would provide political opportunities to all classes. With this combination of social forces, legal social equality emerged. Like Brazil, Mexico, which had seen great violence in earlier decades, achieved independence with almost no bloodshed, but in the next few years bitter conflict among competing leaders resulted in the execution of Iturbide in 1824.

Simón Bolívar and, to a much lesser extent, José San Martín led the largest and most violent revolutions. As early as 1806–1807, the combination of increased demands from the metropole and its concomitant weakness had created restiveness among creoles in Spanish South America. This desire for self-rule had become most ambitious in Argentina; and by May 1810, Buenos Aires threw off European control but could not extend its influence. Only in reaction to the Argentinian push did Paraguay also declare independence. Nonetheless, the idea of independence resonated in Venezuela. Although an impetus for change existed, the involvement of Simón Bolívar proved to be key, as he would lead a series of victorious military expeditions. His importance is shown in the conquest of Peru, the real stalwart in allegiance to Spain. Many of its residents represented the Spanish government in the new world, and military action was necessary to subdue it. While San Martín was successful elsewhere in Latin America, Bolívar's military acumen was necessary to achieve this victory in Peru and cement the victory of the patriot movement in 1819. Some Spanish resistance continued until 1824. In addition to Bolívar's role, the movement's growth outside the creoles to include a broad swath of "Americans" was essential for success (see Map 2.1).

Although Mexico and Brazil as constitutional monarchies generally continued to have strong central governments in the wake of independence, Spanish South American countries such as Argentina, Peru, and Colombia turned immediately to some sort of republican government. And Mexico would soon join them in their republican ways. Thus, independence had swept the region, but republicanism and monarchy coexisted. Despite a pan-Spanish movement, this unifying start did not last and eventually many separate countries emerged.

As in the North American colonies and Haiti, revolution was closely associated with independence, but what else was involved? Examining Simón Bolívar's views and actions helps us comprehend the ideological goals of the new countries where he was active. As the preeminent politician and military leader in South America, he espoused ideas very important to the revolutionary movement. First, he apparently relied on Montesquieu's theory that history, culture, morality, education, and geography—in fact all those aspects of a country's character—prescribed the proper balance between order and freedom. He held England but more explicitly North America to be a place where a perfect democracy could exist. Describing

MAP 2.1 *Revolutionary Latin America.*

Along with San Martín, Bolívar campaigned vigorously over a five-year span to liberate Spanish Latin America.

North America as protected by her seas, especially prosperous, extraordinarily virtuous, and "nourished by freedom," Bolívar insisted that these advantages allowed it more strength and shared values so that it could not be a model for Spanish South America that lacked some of these characteristics.

Even while advocating democracy for the young United States, he noted that "although in many respects that nation is unique in the history of the human race—it is a miracle, I repeat, that a system as weak and complex as federalism [decentralized power] ever managed to guide it through circumstances as an individualized and centralized republic."[1] Here Bolívar expressed his amazement that weak central government could produce good results, even in the most promising circumstances.

Bolívar saw sovereignty required first independence and then, like the North Americans and in theory the French, it would be connected to the entire population. In fact, he continued, "it is our very equality, which we do have, that is part of the reason Latin America cannot allow a weak state and wide political participation ...." In fact, what Bolívar meant by equality was "racial": "our people are not European, nor North American, but are closer to a blend of African and American than an emanation from Europe, for even Spain herself lacks European identify because of her African blood, her institutions, and her character. It is impossible to say with certainty to which human family we belong. Most of the indigenous people have been annihilated."[2] This equality enabled all to aspire to and even demand the benefits of society. Yet this political equality was composed of a mixed population with no single racial stratum. For Bolívar, this challenged any unified government.

Bolívar's notion of borders provides further insight into his conception of national sovereignty. Although he himself wanted to consolidate northern Spanish America in a nation to be called "Gran Colombia," he generally opposed very large countries. Despite all the similarities among the newly liberated colonies, as well as Bolívar's pan-American role in combating Spanish rule, he saw these countries as too different in history and political and economic systems to be easily combined. Moreover, distances and size made one country difficult at best. Did Bolívar believe consolidation difficult because these regions were, in fact, different nations? If, as discussed below, nationalism includes ethnicity and history, the answer must be no. Bolívar seems to have considered administrative viability the principal justification for different countries in South America.

Not surprisingly, Bolívar's vision of the political arrangements for South America was completely different since he regarded South America to have much less favorable conditions, internally and externally, than had the thirteen colonies. In South America, the change in status from colonies without local governmental institutions to independent nations had been sudden. Leaders lacked experience and resources, and few people possessed skills like those of the North Americans. And Bolívar noted in 1819 that in fact Venezuela had already enacted the "rights of man, the freedom to work, think, speak, and write"; but he did not believe that the people were ready for them.[3] He then pointed out that France had had fourteen centuries of monarchical rule to give it stability before it embarked on revolution.

Bolívar thus held that control, "infinitely firm and infinitely delicate," was necessary to manage this heterogeneous society, and the weight of his thinking fell on the difference in race between North and South America.[4] With this belief in a relatively undifferentiated society, Bolívar helped craft the political system that he proposed for the Gran Colombian constitution of 1826. Starting with political equality, he intended to guarantee popular sovereignty, social liberty, individual security, property rights, and social equality. This draft for a constitution also abolished slavery and disestablished religion. The constitution further called for a legislature, courts, and a theoretically weak executive, along with a weak president. Bolívar had consistently opposed monarchs who, in his view, could single-handedly make war. All that said, the executive, including his own successor, possessed appointment powers that undermined voting rights and citizen participation. This was no accident; instead the provision sprang from his more firmly held belief that a strong executive was necessary to lead a poor, uneducated, racially intermixed population. And, in fact, even though the union of all of Gran Colombia was not achieved, Bolívar eventually ruled in a somewhat dictatorial manner.

Reinforcing Bolívar's commitment to a strong executive was his devotion to the ideas of Jean-Jacques Rousseau, who believed that only small, homogeneous societies could function without powerful leadership. Although Rousseau was known for his egalitarian ideas, he distrusted difference and heterogeneity and prescribed a powerful central government for large countries, whose populations he assumed had many differences. Specifically, Poland needed a powerful executive; tiny Corsica did not. Consequently, Bolívar, though he advocated for a weak administration, actually created a strong executive position that he personally would occupy. He knew the power he would derive from the constitution that he proposed only fed cynicism and hostility. Indeed, eventually his constituency tired of him, and in 1830, a broken man, he left his position and died shortly thereafter.

Bolívar's ruminations further continued the debate about legal equality and functional democracy. He eclipsed the North Americans and French by proposing a personal equality far beyond what these countries could contemplate; on the other hand, he retreated regarding democracy because an egalitarian society could not accept nearly as much political action as he believed necessary. Elsewhere, Latin Americans followed a similar route—more equality and lower political participation—than in the North Atlantic. Still, independence from the mother countries proved to be an important achievement.

In regard to the development of the revolutionary idea, Bolívar's actions and ideas surely deepened the link between republicanism and independence. In short, both human rights and democracy continued to spread in this era throughout the Atlantic world, as a system of symbols and often as a reality, but usually in Europe as a result of political evolution and reform rather than violent revolution. Soon revolutions would become even more firmly connected to novel ideas about nationhood.

Nationalist revolution

To perceive how the modern notion of nationalism became incorporated in the revolutionary lexicon, the ideology, its origins, and its acceptance must be understood, before examining its use to overthrow governments. No political concept developed in the modern world has proven more attractive than nationalism, but at best it remains an elusive term. To understand its emergence in the nineteenth century, one must begin with the political arrangement of Europe where, in fact, political nationalism received most of its initial impetus. Forms of cultural nationalism were emerging in Japan and elsewhere, but not yet in the political realm.

Europe proved in the nineteenth century to be very fertile ground for nationalism, an ideology with few or no precedents in European governments before that century. In fact, dominating this European map were empires, large conglomerations of territories that included numerous, often disparate, language or cultural groups. Only the monarch united such areas, which in many cases in the future emerged as separate entities. Many had been previously independent. A few small countries maintained independence, but even these were not yet nations as the term would come to be used. Prerevolutionary France, a highly integrated society, symbolically came together only in the person of the king. The parlements that played such an integral role, including the dominant Parisian one, remained regional organizations. Similarly the delegates to the Estates General arrived from electorates that were often defined in histories of independent or relatively independent fiefdoms or countries. On June 17, 1789, the body renamed itself the National Assembly, making sovereignty adhere to the "nation."

Royal dynasties, representing European territories, dominated (see Map 2.2). To be sure, proto-nationalist feelings motivated debates on culture, but inhabitants of such countries had no political focal point other than the monarch or emperor. One obvious exception was the new United States which, after adoption of its new constitution in 1789, had a national government with a president and a Congress, though states continued to assert local rights in one form or another during much of the nineteenth century. In short, like human rights and democracy, many countries came to embrace nationalism, but this development was unexpected, not evident to contemporaries in advance, and its enormous success hardly inevitable.

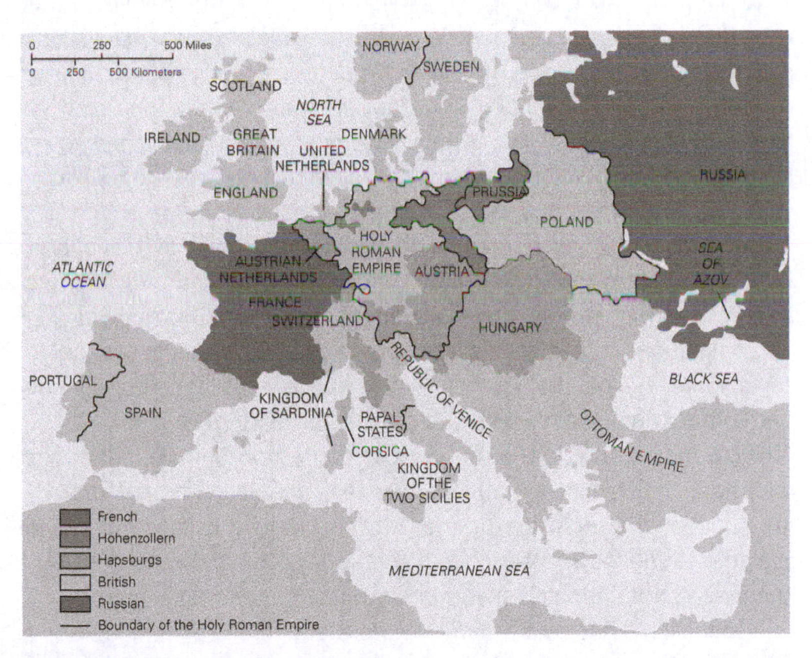

MAP 2.2 *Dynastic Europe in 1789.*

On the eve of the French Revolution, continental Europe was mainly ruled by kings. The English monarchs had united the British Isles; the Hapburgs ruled over much of central Europe, including the Holy Roman Empire; the Prussian Hohenzollerns were extending their authority as were the Russian tsars to the south and east of Moscow; and the Bourbon family had monarchs ruling two major countries – France and Spain.

To understand the acceptance of nationalism requires a more thorough explanation of the concept's components. Lloyd Kramer's superb study of European nationalism provides an excellent guide. Noting that nationalists "always unite strong claims to defend specific geographic territories, specific historical memories, and the specific right to a sovereign state," he lists a number of aspects: people must constantly be educated to hold notions of their own nationality; nationalism establishes its group's characteristics by stressing differences from other societies; nationalism develops an emotional, religious-like passion, and like gender, parafamily, and race, creates aspects of personal identity.[5] Moreover, over time "blood," meaning a deep ahistorical lineage, became associated with some nationalities. Nationalities of this type essentially depended on a past so distant but also so seemingly certain that the descendants believed that they were naturally linked through ethnic identities. The apotheosis of this latter tendency may be found among the fascists and chauvinistic nationalists of the late nineteenth and twentieth centuries; in contrast, most multicultural countries in the western hemisphere have embraced nationalism without claiming a single racial ancestry. And France and America, which had already achieved nationalism, constructed a looser nationalism more like that of their neighbors.

But nationalism, whether "old" or new, had as its basic goal to create a state that collected all those of near identity within its boundaries. As historical continuity appeared central to the identities, nations sought to become sovereign geographical units that could consolidate the people and their living space together. Segregation from others and internal unification became major demands.

Although by the last century most contemporaries experienced their national identity as intrinsic and real, scholars, more struck by the sudden and rapid emergence of this belief, have continued to seek the cause for its creation and spread over the last two centuries. Theories about nationalism abound, but no consensus exists.

Nationalism has had many interpreters. Benedict Anderson's *Imagined Communities: Reflections on the Origin and Spread of Nationalism* is the most influential and widely cited work.[6] Relying on the general growth of literacy and a much larger reading public, Anderson argued that a consequent spread of print, coupled with national and international markets that induced individuals to read about developments such as exchange rates, encouraged the use of national languages, and a press network and shared literature abetted this consolidation. A reading public emerged that was easy to reach through the appeal of nationalist rhetoric. Moreover, as this group was bonded by language, particularist rather than universal conceptions might come to prevail. Historian Charles Clark produced another version of the same argument for the North American colonies. Relying in particular on the press, he argued that nationalism emerged from colonial newspapers' sharing of news. Covering American events in their sheets, they constructed a far more united community of colonies than had earlier existed and prepared for a particular "imagined" community, the United States.[7]

In fact, country-centered explanations of the rise of nationalism may be most convincing. As earlier noted, France was probably the most integrated country in Europe on the eve of the revolution. Building upon an explanation by historian David Bell, I would suggest that understanding French nationalism is important because other countries were induced to follow its example. From the morass of the seventeenth-century religious wars and noble resistance came the enormous extension of power under Louis XIV, including a massive increase in his ability to wage war and achieve some geopolitical success. In addition, the Sun King quieted dissent through his suppression of religious difference and his creation of the Académie française to standardize the French language. In the eighteenth century, even though dissent rose, many occurrences intersected to unify France and make nationalism possible. Among these were the immense growth of the periodical press after 1750, the increasing safety of travel after the 1720s, the state assuming much more responsibility for care of the poor, and the growth of trade networks extending inward from the Atlantic ports. Political turmoil increased, but so did state integration. Later in the revolution itself, news and direct announcement of the news (in local dialects and languages, when necessary) made its way through the countryside. In fact, the French Revolution became possible because a nation had been gradually constructed. Revolution meant taking control of the state in the name of the people rather than the king. The revolution also helped to make France an extraordinary national workshop of political education, which continued in the public schools well into the twentieth century. Furthermore, as many historians have noted, the success of France's army, if not its revolution, encouraged international emulation. This military threat also pushed other countries to reorganize and gain internal support to avoid being swallowed by the French Revolution.

In any case, nationalism as a movement rushed through Europe and beyond as a mighty torrent. Some movements were reformist; others sought revolution; many were opportunistic. In the first three quarters of the eighteenth century, few places remained untouched; yet by 1875 only a few European countries had achieved the levels of integration they would in subsequent decades.

If nationalism was so irresistible and omnipresent, why did it achieve so little success, at least at first? Here two answers are necessary. The first and most obvious is repression. The most vulnerable dynasty in Europe was the enormous Austrian Empire, which included south German lands as well as Slavic areas along the Adriatic and most of Italy. Metternich, prime minister of Austria, recognized that his country, weakened during the era of the French Revolution and composed of ethnic groups increasingly motivated by nascent nationalism, needed to thwart revolutionary aspirations. Against the odds, he turned Tsar Alexander I, earlier a supporter of nationalist aspirations, into an inveterate foe of these new threats. Together they systematically crushed nascent revolutions and uprisings. Moreover, nationalists were their own worst enemies. Although each "nation" in theory would occupy a separate space, this was all self-defining and lacked any mechanism to secure agreement. Thus, national groups coveted each other's lands. Particularly during the revolution of 1848–1849, the most serious European political upheaval between the French and Russian Revolutions, various nationalities of the Austrian Empire quarreled, making it possible for the Viennese regime to survive until after the First World War. Although Italy pulled free before the world war and the Austrian Empire lost other lands, it remained viable until the peace treaty at Versailles in 1919.

Nonetheless, nationalism was a vital force, and independence and unification certainly had in the nineteenth century occurred in Denmark, Belgium, Greece, Switzerland, and Italy. Germany emerged from a consolidation of Prussia with an assortment of other German principalities and kingdoms. Revolutionaries helped propel the creation of this large, potent central European country. The vital force, however, was Otto von Bismarck, Prussia's prime minister, who cynically hijacked nationalistic goals to build a state without either the participation or the goals of many insurgents. In contrast, Italy, by virtue of its size, history, and population, remained the most important prize for the revolutionaries. In 1815, Italy had been only a geographical expression, and this had been the case for much of the previous millennium. By 1871, it had achieved most of its current boundaries. In order to understand the ideas that propelled such momentous change, this chapter first charts the course of unification and then examines the ideological contribution of Giuseppe Mazzini and Giuseppe Garibaldi, the two most prominent figures in the Italian revolutionary pantheon. Rather than broadly surveying the actors, this focus highlights the ideas and actions of these individuals, who were even more important than the Hungarian Lajos Kossuth, the closest competitor for fame and recognition. Through these Italians, we can begin to understand facets of this complex movement of nationalism.

Not surprisingly, after the successful unification of Italy and rise in the country's international profile, contemporary historians from Italy lionized Mazzini and Garibaldi. As integral to the noble founding myth of the nation, they were generally immune from criticism. The next generation of scholars in the twentieth century, however, turned against the two revolutionaries. Perhaps influenced by the internal weaknesses of contemporary Italy and its descent into fascism in the 1920s, this group denigrated the contribution of the two former heroes. Among historians writing in English, the incredibly prolific historian Denis Mack Smith most prominently put forward this interpretation. Scholars like Mack focused on the Piedmont government, especially its long serving prime minister Camillo Benso, the Count of Cavour. In this account, Cavour was the puppet master, responsible for all the meaningful steps toward national unification. Arguing that the critical subject comprised the negotiations and diplomatic maneuvers between Piedmont and the other "Great Powers," historians like Mack generally called Cavour's actions *realpolitik* and emphasized that self-interest not idealism provided the impetus to create Italy. These machinations could not possibly provide the foundation for a strong national state. But as the following description of unification shows, the scholarly pendulum has swung back to a more balanced position that acknowledges the efforts and implies a more positive long-term impact of both the politicians and revolutionaries.

After the defeat of Napoleon in 1815, the Italian peninsula housed a dozen monarchies, more or less under the control of the Austrian government, except for the Papal States and the Kingdom of Savoy, consisting of Piedmont and Sardinia located north and west of the peninsula. The Congress of Vienna had left this land with a modicum of power to serve as a buffer between the Austrian-dominated areas and France, defeated but still a superpower in Europe (see Map 2.3).

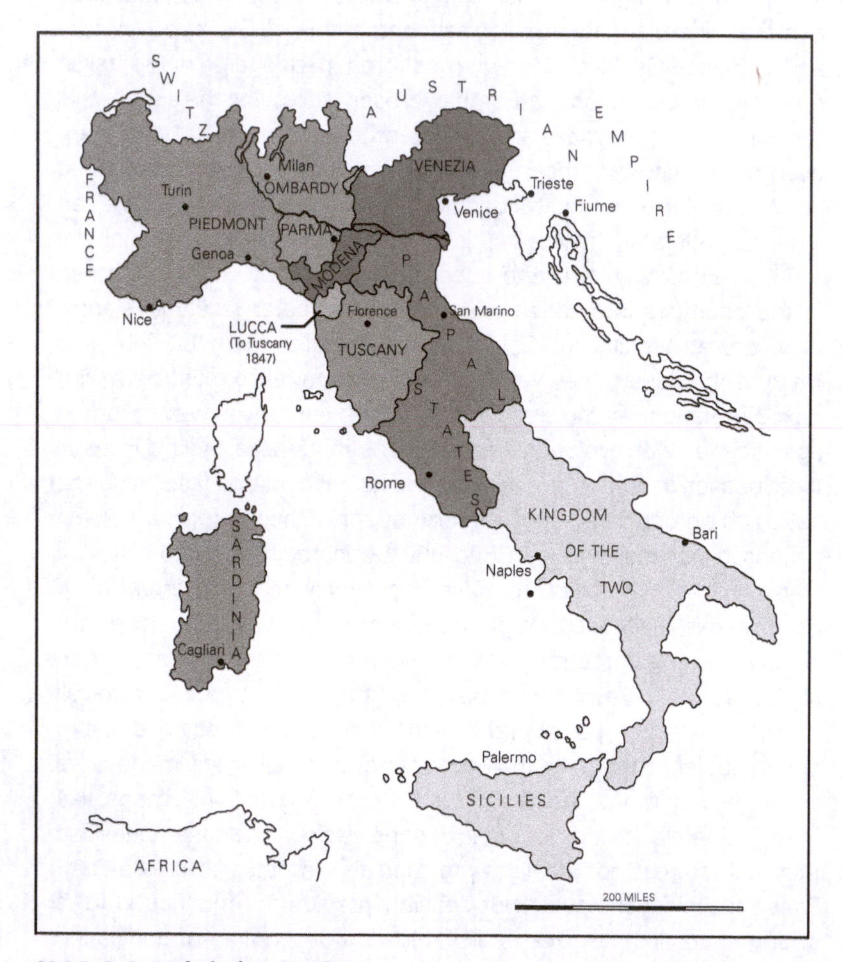

MAP 2.3 *Italy before Unification.*

Into this political situation came Giuseppe Mazzini (b. Genoa 1805), who early was drawn into radical politics and made his mark in 1831 by founding Young Italy whose primary goal was Italian unification. This organization made him the most visible of a group of Italian nationalists. From France, then London, he plotted to whip up enthusiasm for nationalism. His writings and his activities sparked support among many who followed his beliefs, but all their attempted coups failed. Nonetheless, they surely frightened the post-1815 governments. Events well beyond his control provided a gigantic new stage for Mazzini and his ideas. In 1848, Paris exploded with revolution, founding a new French republic and ousting king Louis-Philippe, who himself had gained the throne in an 1830 revolution. As the uprising of 1848 echoed throughout Europe, Rome, revolting against an unpopular Pope, installed Mazzini as one of three triumvirs. This republican government was short-lived, but the movement received enormous publicity. Moreover, Giuseppe Garibaldi (1807–1882) emerged as its hero, and his daring and flair attracted attention and invigorated Mazzini's ideas with a new appeal.

At this point in 1852, Cavour began efforts which likewise were central to the achievements that followed. Comprehending the prime minister's actions, which were not inspired by nationalism, one needs to recall that the mandate of kingship included enhancing the realm. Enlarging one's country by taking another's territory remained an important means of doing that. Various provocations could serve as causes, and monarchs often relied on flimsy reasons, real or manufactured, to justify aggression. Both Cavour and the king Victor Emmanuel, who also was a recent convert to reform, believed in liberalism—secularism, free trade, progress, and constitutional and parliamentary government. Thus, Cavour was open to working with the nationalists and their broader politics and even advocating national unity—though primarily he wished Piedmont's king to emerge as head of a much enlarged realm.

To increase Piedmont's power meant weakening Austria's authority in Italy; and for that, Cavour turned to an alliance with the French emperor Napoleon III, who had come to power by toppling the government installed by the 1848 revolution. Together they pushed east from Piedmont, easily overturning most of the governments there in the North during the next decade. But Napoleon worried about the rise of radicalism, withdrew in 1860 from the alliance, leaving unification only half complete.

Mazzini's political ideas were coming to fruition, but it was Garibaldi's involvement that attempted a much bigger success. Following the withdrawal of the French, Cavour pushed forward militarily to the east to create a larger state in northern Italy. More or less on his own, Garibaldi assembled a ragtag force which he called "The Thousand" and invaded Sicily. Advancing rapidly across the island, he quickly engineered the defeat and retreat of Neapolitan forces. All this pushed Cavour to drive south to link up with Garibaldi in order to avoid this uncontrollable force gaining too much power. Although the Venetian and the Papal states still resisted, they soon fell in line. In 1870, the entire Italian boot was consolidated under the rule of King Victor Emmanuel. While many Italian nationalists would likely have preferred a republic, it was impossible to reject the embrace of Piedmont-Sardinia, a highly dynamic and surely the most powerful indigenous military force on the peninsula.

Recent scholars divide credit for the initiative among Cavour, Mazzini, and Garibaldi. Clearly Mazzini's ideas triumphed, though under a monarch and in less secular manner than he would have preferred. And Garibaldi's impetuous attack attained nationalist goals far more quickly.

The symbolic and actual contributions of Mazzini, the intellectual, and Garibaldi, the warrior, to notions of national unity in Italy and beyond her borders can scarcely be overstated. Though certainly not typical, they provide an extraordinary lens for understanding the idea and culture of this nationalistic movement. In fact, their ideas were important because dynasties elsewhere also had to confront such dangerous notions that might delegitimize their authority. Although Mazzini was known for his advocacy of the nation-state, he clearly indicated that such nations were but an intermediary step to the brotherhood of man. He wished to harness aggressive nationalism to come to the assistance of mankind.[8] In fact, those who attained nationhood had a duty to help others achieve the same.

But first was the nation. Mazzini's article, "Foreign Despotism to Civilize a People: Italy, Austria, and the Pope" (1855), stands as one of his most expansive statements regarding his vision of the nation. Objecting to ameliorations offered by the Austrians designed to satisfy and quell Italian nationalist ambitions, Mazzini demanded that "It is the *Soul* of the Italian Nation—its thought, mission, and conscience—that is at stake." Italians deserved the right to "a national union with other millions of brothers ... who speak the same language and tread the same earth. All of them were cradled in their infancy with the same national songs, strengthened in their youth by the same sun, inspired by the same historical memories and the same sources of literary genius." "Country, liberty, brotherhood, vocation ...,"[9] all these were necessary. Elsewhere Mazzini underlined his core belief in the power of shared history, culture, and territory:

> We are a people of 21 or 22 million, known from time immemorial by the same name, as the people of Italy. We are enclosed by clear natural limits—the sea and the highest mountains in Europe. We also speak the same language, with a variety of dialects that differ from each other less than the Scotch and the English. More generally, we have the same creeds, manners, and habits with differences not greater than those which in France, the most homogeneous country on earth, distinguish the Basques from the Bretons.[10]

Not only did Italians have much in common, but also much about which to boast:

> We are the proud guardians of the noblest European tradition in politics, science, and the arts. We have twice unified Humanity: first through the Rome of the emperors; then again through the Rome of the popes, although the latter betrayed their mission. Not even our calumniators deny that we are gifted with active and brilliant faculties. Finally, we richly possess every source of material well-being, which, if we became free to cooperate fraternally, could make us happy and offer great prospects to our sister nations.[11]

Despite this positive notion of nationhood that viewed it a building block toward the welfare of man, not all nations qualified. Not only were the Austrians different than the Italians, but they are a "people of conquerors." Correcting himself, Mazzini noted that the Austrians never conquered anything, but usurped what they had through treaties and marriage. They only maintained themselves by "spreading terror," relying on "brute force," and using treacherous spies.[12] Like others of his time, Mazzini was condescending toward non-Western peoples. Noting that Asia had once populated Italy, he advocated a "moral mission" for Italians to transform Asian religions, industry, and agriculture. In reference to other Western nations' conquest of colonies around the world, Mazzini inferred that "Italy was once the most powerful colonizer of the world, and thus should not lose out on this wonderful new movement."[13] In his view, the best target was North Africa. Mazzini thus amended the new notion of sovereignty articulated in American independence movements which focused on acceptance of all residents without particular reference to their origins. His view was Italy for Italians whose history rested within peninsular soil. Although this approach would later prove exclusionary and oppressive, this was not Mazzini's goal, which was much more to rally a people.

With unifying Italy his main focus, Mazzini tried to establish programs in a narrow path between the competing ideologies of the period. He opposed socialism and directly quarreled with Marx about it, undermining the possibility of allying with Italian left-wing political groups. He did not, however, oppose social programs. Decrying self-help as entirely insufficient, he argued for a just wage for labor. A right to private property should exist, but all profits from commerce should be divided according to how much labor each individual puts into the product. Governments should provide social services, infrastructure, and the creation of a national capital fund available to all.

Mazzini also shied away from liberalism in its libertarian form which he equated with license. He preferred that the bill of rights be limited to necessities of life. One observes hesitations about impulsive behavior like that which Bolívar had also decried. But rather than imposing a strong controlling government, Mazzini tried to constrain the selfish demands of individuals. Opposing slavery and formal class divisions, he supported national sovereignty with full democracy.

In a career of writing and organizing, Mazzini spent little of his adult life in Italy and believed change inextricably linked to action. In fact, in 1832, he wrote a tract, "Rules for the Conduct of Guerrilla Bands."[14] Rather than a code of ethics, this was a guide to strategy, presaging similar works by Cuban and Vietnamese revolutionaries. Although Mazzini did not favor assassinating leaders, he was more than willing to contemplate stealth. Guerrillas should not engage in direct battles, but should rely on inflicting as much damage as possible with special attention to offense. He urged ambushes, leaking false information, and holding one's fire until the enemy made its position clear. Almost two centuries later, it seems unimaginable that this advocate of guerrilla war was allowed by authorities to live openly in London. Indeed, while the French and Americans made a revolution, unsure whether they would meet violent resistance, Mazzini, abroad as he usually was, held no such concerns for himself and could personally advocate such tactics without fear of intervention from authorities there or from other European countries. In contrast, over a century later, when Che Guevara outlined guerrilla war, he wrote from the mountains of Cuba and the jungles of South America.

Even the intellectual Mazzini required violence to establish nationalism and make a revolution. In fact, when Mazzini realized Garibaldi's capabilities, he embraced the colorful, daring aggression that Garibaldi inflicted and represented. Indeed, Mazzini insisted that he had been looking for such a man.

Garibaldi did much to popularize and legitimate violence as part of the nationalist effort. He built his image on Mazzini's theory of the nation, which was highly congruent with the Romanticism that was the rage in Europe. Disseminated by the German writer J.G. Herder, this new cultural idea focused on the notion that each people had a special character and a people's genius must connect to its roots. Mazzini's emphasis on nationalism that linked ethnicity and history to a particular people thus appeared modern to contemporaries following the latest intellectual trends. It should, however, be emphasized that Herder did not view these people in racial terms, as would later fascists, but rather simply as the result of history and experience. Garibaldi was that heroic figure emerging from the Italians. Garibaldi appealed to other elements of Romanticism, including images of the warrior triumphing against all odds and the unconventional hero untrammeled by conventions.

In fact, as historian Lucy Riall compellingly argues, Garibaldi's image and message, which created a large following, were carefully managed by both Mazzini and Garibaldi himself. Several elements contributed to the nationalist message fashioned by Mazzini, which sought to change personal values. As the press followed the exploits of Garibaldi, his actions and publicity incorporated hypermasculinity and a love of family into the nationalist image. Garibaldi's good looks especially made him, as the revolution's symbol, appear the nineteenth-century version of a highly masculine movie star. Moreover, because Garibaldi mainly fought with volunteers, he added a strong sense of nationalism as the province of all and emanated a spirit of intense sharing among Italians. All these characteristics of his public presence shaped the national community in antielitist and male-dominated bonds of comradeship reinforced by military action. Linked to this gendered vision was a reinforcement of the patriarchy. Interestingly, Garibaldi's willingness to invoke God and cooperate with the clergy as well as his support of Victor Emmanuel beginning in 1860 defused the secular and republican messages of Mazzini, who also found himself tempering his earlier positions. According to Mazzini, God had created Italy but became hostile to the Church. Nonetheless, in this period in Italy, old elites and new notions could coexist.[15]

In summary, however, Garibaldi did more to legitimate nationalist rhetoric than to elaborate it. As a quintessential romantic hero, he enhanced the alignment of the revolution with unification more than with the philosophical notions. Further, Garibaldi's exploits breathed emotion and passion, also romantic values, into the already overheated rhetoric found in Mazzini's passionate support for a unified nation. Above all, Garibaldi promoted the idea of national sovereignty. See Map 2.4 for the proliferation of nation-states.

> Nationalism is still strong in the contemporary world. Is it defined as it once was at its beginning?

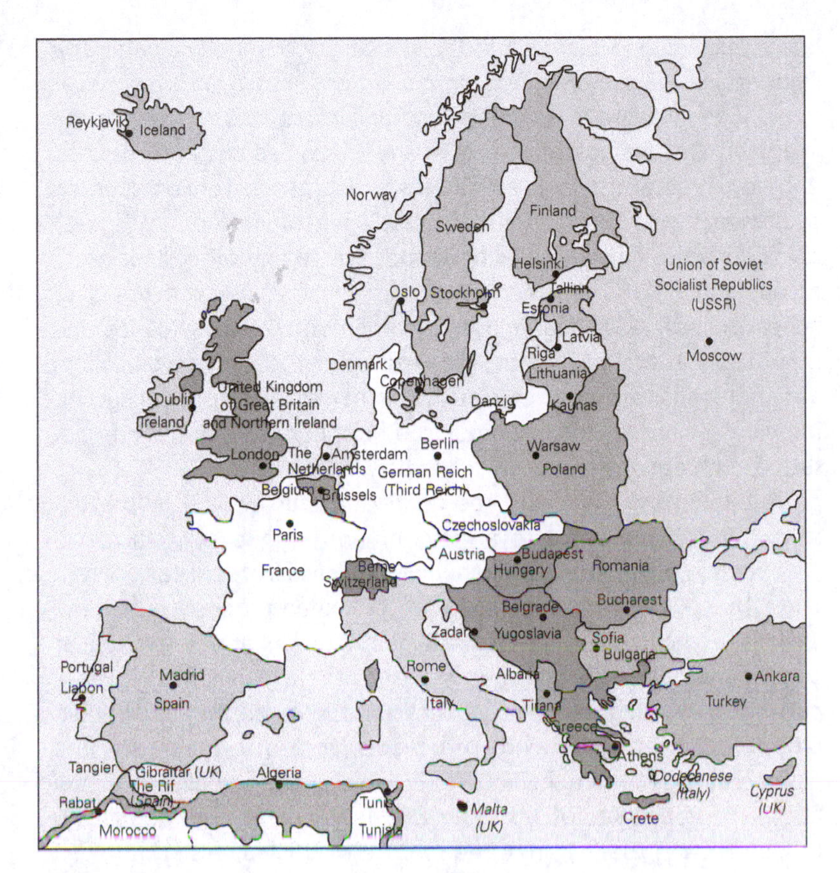

MAP 2.4 *Europe in 1939: A Wealth of Nations.*

Marxism

The Americans and the French had found violence proved necessary to defend their revolutions, even though the Americans must have been uncertain about how much war would be necessary and at least at first the French in 1789 were unlikely to have even considered the possibility. From the beginning, Mazzini planned for violence. Karl Marx and his colleague Friedrich Engels also believed violence and revolution inextricable one from the other. Having to defend or assert one's goals made violence and the necessary change like parts of a DNA chain—ineluctably linked. In his lifetime, however, Marx never actually participated in anything resembling the class revolution he imagined. Despite not being part of a revolution as this book defines it, he must be examined because his script, or the version adopted by others, motivated and instructed generations of "Marxist" revolutionaries. In part, by living longer than many other "socialist" competitors, Marx became the predominant voice of a brand of radical politics. Additionally, in an environment where evidence and proof were in the ascendant, Marx linked the idea of revolution to a comprehensive theory of history. Rather than simply pitting one morality against another, he could use a theory to show a brighter future, with options that drew followers.

Understanding Marx requires contextualization. Even before the revolution in France, the royal government, in extending its reach, was replacing the church in providing necessary services for the poor. Although the revolutionary elite defended property rights and did little, compared to its political goals, to link the revolution to social benefits, laborers in Paris in particular saw relief payments as part of their hopes. As the Jacobins seized power, they more than others embraced these kinds of policies, at least symbolically, and greatly expanded them. In fact, in 1793 the Jacobins published a new Declaration of Rights of Man and Citizen which, though continuing to guarantee property in three separate articles, also promised education and public relief, depicted as a "sacred debt. Society owes maintenance to unfortunate citizens, either procuring work for them or in providing the means of existence for those who are unable to work." And in fact, for a while the Jacobins experimented with price controls. Furthermore, they balanced their maintenance of private property by providing help for the indigent. Of course, this plan reified property as much or likely more than it helped the poor.

Nonetheless, the social question had emerged, and the Babeuf plot (1796) appears to have taken it much further. Because the actions and motives of Gracchus Babeuf and his allies were only recounted many decades later and remain murky, we cannot be sure of the details. But Babeuf, whom the eminent late historian R.B. Rose called "the first Revolutionary Communist," may have been Marx's first serious predecessor.[16] Rose was hardly the first one to make this connection, as the Russian communists had already anointed Babeuf as the first of their ilk. According to Filippo Buonarroti, a co-conspirator who only in 1828 published details of the plot, Babeuf and his allies planned to socialize the labor of citizens and provide to all a necessary subsistence of food, medicine, shelter, and other basics of life. Further, elected economic administrators would arrange the economy to improve production and distribute goods across a wide area. All this would require a violent seizure of power as well as a slow transition from Jacobinism to this new economic plan. In fact, an uprising would begin with an explosion of violence, and strong coercive measures to achieve widespread compliance would follow. Even with this scenario, Rose concluded by noting the approach was likely more Jacobin than communistic.

Whether these retrospective details were accurate, the French government had taken this conspiracy seriously and sentenced Babeuf and some of his followers to death. And the plot matters little in terms of understanding Marx because other socialist ideas were circulating in the postrevolutionary world, competing of course with Jacobin ideas that also called for a more egalitarian world, forced by revolution if necessary. (Communism and socialism were used almost interchangeably in this era except that the former often had a more radical connotation than the latter. Only after the Bolshevik revolution of 1917 would these terms become more fixed in their meanings with communism identified with Bolshevik beliefs and socialism opposed.) Sorting through the differences that varied from place to place over time goes well beyond the confines of this chapter, except to note that the socialist side mostly called for radical reform to end or sharply curtail private property and to redistribute and manage it far more fairly whereas communists called for more violent methods of social change led by a dominant party. Among these socialists were radical trade unionists, anarchists, and libertarians whose solution was a state with limited power. Needless to say, these were passionate groups with strong opinions, so internecine battles often trumped the efforts to battle either the state or capitalism.

Within this fantastic swirl of revolutionary ideas were a few notable plans for socialist societies that presaged the modern communal efforts that would much later flourish during the 1960s and 1970s. But in the early nineteenth century there were those who wished to create a separate socialist world and escape the oppression of capitalism, all without benefit of a revolution. Marx later called these efforts utopian socialist, partly to differentiate them from his belief about the scientific nature of his plans, and scholars have used the label, accepting as well that Marx's approach surely included a greater amount of empirical data.

Although the impact and spread of the utopian communities was limited, the plans of Charles Fourier, the most intense progenitor of this approach who inspired some brief experimental communities, deserve mention. Fourier's ideas provided a sense of a planned use of socialism to liberate humans. He labeled his experiments "phalansteries" whose ideal population for each location was 1,800. His basic goal was that everyone would work hard, but always at tasks that they wanted to do. His ideal size for communities came from calculating passions; that population would allow the residents to satisfy their different sexual desires. Because Fourier could never leave well enough alone, he provided that elders, who no longer participated, would be eligible to hear all the gossip from the others' love life.

Clearly, Fourier's largest problem was having the most disagreeable jobs performed. For that he had many solutions. Because young children like to play together in the dirt, he envisioned grouping them into "hordes" for garbage removal. And those whose passions might turn into vices would be directed toward productive work: the bloodthirsty would be butchers or hunters. What Fourier attempted to capture in his scheme was an answer to Rousseau's quest to unite civilization with personal freedom; Rousseau had declared that a small homogeneous society was necessary. For believers, Fourier provided an answer that glorified diversity and freedom through socialism (or near socialism as he provided a minor and exceptional role for private property).

Social, economic, and political developments induced as well as supported this variety of radical republican and socialistic notions. At the time of the French Revolution, only England was undergoing the industrial revolution, but in the early nineteenth century, Western Europe was beginning to experience the same economic expansion. While the growth of factories then has been overstated, the number of cities with a large impoverished laboring poor was very substantial and rapidly increasing, especially after the first quarter of the nineteenth century. In these developments radicals found material to elaborate social and political remedies far beyond what the traditional monarchs, who regained most of their power after Napoleon's defeat in 1815, were willing even to contemplate. Moreover, although such revolutionaries were widely unwelcome or worse, havens for them existed in England, but also in France under king Louis-Philippe (who ruled from 1830 to 1848). Circumstance and community were a lively petri dish for radical movements.

Emerging from this European intellectual ferment was Karl Marx (1818–1883), born in Trier in the Prussian Rhineland, who made an impact on revolution and politics that is both difficult to overstate and to evaluate. Marx wrote so many of his works with Friedrich Engels (1820–1895) that it is often difficult to separate their thoughts. Many historians simply cite Marx when it would be more accurate though clumsy to indicate both. For efficiency's sake, this chapter refers to Marx. Another difficulty is that, despite Marx's often desultory work habits, he wrote so much, in so many different venues, that even seventy-five years ago, the eminent political scientist Samuel Beer opined: "To reduce Marxism to a single, coherent body is far from an easy task. The term refers to … Marx and Engels, whose ideas quite naturally changed and developed from one work to another. It also includes the interpretations and restatements of these views by the host of disciples …."[17] And, in fact, recent interpretations continue to provide stunningly little congruence in approach or focus.

Although social and intellectual change abounded, the young Marx was not at first interested. In fact, the repression of Prussian authorities probably inhibited any public airing of social concerns. In the same way that the eighteenth-century philosophes had often used fiction to express political views indirectly, German students pursued philosophy. Before Marx began to focus on social change in 1843, he had become a philosophy student, entranced by philosopher Georg F. W. Hegel and his interpretation of history. This eminent scholar had first taken issue with the empiricist, fact-based philosophy that was preeminent in France and especially with the Scottish philosopher David Hume who argued that theories must start with irreducible nuggets of data. Hume was so nominalist that he completely distrusted generalizations. In contrast, Hegel argued that "facts" existed in a continuum, and an individual's knowledge of a piece of information was meaningless, unless he understood how it fit in a logical chain. For Hegel, concepts advanced according to a clear dialectic: hurtling in one direction (thesis), a reaction is created (antithesis), whose interaction creates progress and a new fusion of ideas (synthesis). The organization of information revealed its meaning. Once synthesis arrived, then the process recommenced. Young Hegelians saw this as the progress of a spirit that embodied the growth and development of a freer, better system. "Right Hegelians" sought a more nationalist end, while "Left Hegelians" such as Marx put greater emphasis on a more observable world.

Marx came to accept the dialectic, renamed it dialectical materialism, and invested it with economic evolution; instead of ideas, of course, he focused upon the economic development unfolding in front of him. He viewed the struggle as not between ideas but between social classes. Their dynamics and elements lay at the heart of Marx's theory—he argued that societies passed through a number of stages: Asiatic state system, slavery, feudalism, capitalism, and, in the future, communism. Yet the class struggle always occurred between the oppressed and oppressors. The basic conflict begat invention. At the first, all labored to provide necessities, but as acquisition and consumption defined existence, man's ingenuity and innovativeness elevated some above the others. Two classes emerged: those who owned the means of production and those who did not. At first, the two differed little, but eventually owners paid laborers only enough for existence and retained the rest. This immiseration of the workers eventually resulted in a battle between the two sides. Marx then elaborated the end of each stage as a struggle that flared into open warfare only when the organization of the economy had reached its highest level of performance *and* when a new structure of production had been constructed to replace the old.

Even as a philosopher, Marx was by the 1840s fully engaged in a political struggle to remedy the economic ills that he saw. Thus, he turned his research more specifically toward the current stage of capitalism in the dialectic which he saw also as the final era of transformation leading to socialism. For Marx, this penultimate stage emerged because the discovery of America, trade with East

Asia, and colonization had disrupted feudalism. The class currently owning the means of production—the bourgeoisie—took advantage of all these new assets and was exploiting industrial possibilities. In fact, Marxist analyses depend on the proposition that the price of an object for sale rested upon the cost of labor, calculated as the cost of keeping a worker alive and able to procreate (to produce replacements in the labor force) plus the cost of rent, capital, and a decent profit. Although at the inception of an economic era, profits were reasonably moderate, over time the bourgeoisie (owners of the means of production in this period in Marxist terminology) had no choice but to pursue self-interest more and more aggressively. Since labor costs were already at the minimum, this involved increasing investment in machines and other labor and cost-saving devices. All this unfettered competition would result not only in the destruction of all prior economic regimes but also some elements of the bourgeoisie. The petty bourgeoisie, including smaller tradesmen, landlords, shopkeepers, and the like, could not compete because they lacked the capital to match the efficiency of the upper bourgeoisie. They too would sink into the proletariat, as Marx and Engels referred to the industrial working class.

As society fell into two wildly unequal parts, a few capitalists and their political representatives would have to deal with the burgeoning proletariat. Still extant would be a lower strata of tradesmen but because they aspired only to return to former relationships, they would not aid the laborers. Marx and Engels worried most about what they called the lumpenproletariat, the very poorest classes that would inevitably adopt criminal behaviors. In their writings on 1848, Marx and Engels specifically predicted that the bourgeoisie would bribe this class to interfere. Nevertheless, nothing could stop the proletariat which had been created by the advance of capitalism.

The proletariat, by its immiseration and near enslavement, and with the help of educated classes who themselves would be thrown into the proletariat, finally would revolt and throw off the reign of the bourgeoisie. Marx's *Communist Manifesto* clearly indicated that the Communist Party would take a leading role in helping laborers achieve the self-consciousness necessary to achieve all this. Further in this phase, self-interest would create a moral good for all the proletarians because they would act to equalize conditions and end expropriation by the bourgeoisie. Marx argued that all bourgeois values were simply prejudices, just extensions of interest. But the proletariat in revolution would not defend any minority but instead the entire society. It would be the "self-conscious, independent movement of the immense majority, in the interest of the majority."[18] Consequently, all would be liberated, and improvements in the economy equally distributed.

Many questions about the *Communist Manifesto*'s interpretation emerged subsequently, with answers of various sorts provided directly or indirectly by Marx and Engels. Moreover, Marx remained deeply concerned about some elements. Jonathan Sperber in his comprehensive, extraordinarily well-researched biography of Marx noted two issues that Marx raised and seems not to have settled himself.[19] Although Marx was first of all a committed revolutionary, he was seriously involved, as even some of his polemical work evidenced (e.g., class struggle), in securing empirical proof of his positions. Specifically, classical economics, on which Marx depended, predicted the profit margin would decline over time. Although this factor would help to explain the elimination of many merchants, it was not strictly necessary to his theory as Marx could simply have argued that the upper bourgeoisie would simply monopolize whatever profits occurred. Nonetheless, expecting to find this phenomenon of declining profits, he was seriously troubled by his inability to do so. Moreover, Marx could not empirically explain the way that prices were determined. He could not figure out why items might have the same price even though the inputs of labor and materials varied. Without the link between cost of inputs (worker wages, etc.) and price to show that sooner or later labor must receive only subsistence in order for an employer to remain competitive, Marx could not explain why poverty must occur. If prices remained stubbornly high, the proletarianization of the workers, necessary to his theory, would not arrive.

Although Marx expended significant energy regarding these issues in economic theory, he did not explain much of the role of activist organizers. The *Communist Manifesto* described the revolution as a violent takeover by the proletariat whose consciousness had been raised by defectors from the bourgeoisie, but it gave relatively little attention to this process. In fact, the *Manifesto* described a potent logic of class conflict with an inevitable result. Revolutions would come when an intense disconnect existed between the people who held political power and the most oppressed, and thus energized, economic class—which would soon be the proletariat. Consider a massive proletariat opposing a shrinking bourgeoisie. Would not the result simply be an avalanche poised to occur? In this description one cannot find the trigger that begins the revolution.

Many scholars, considering the vast range of Marx's work, have contributed a more compelling interpretation of the place of violent revolution in Marx and Engels's world view. The eminent philosopher and historian Isaiah Berlin asserted that only in *Das Kapital*, first published in 1867, did Marx's ideas come together coherently.[20] First, as also noted in the *Manifesto*, the central purpose of each economic class was its own well-being. For example, the bourgeoisie came into existence as a progressive class proud of overturning feudalism and willing to impose its own network of beliefs in every area. This class saw its values as universal, not contingent, "eternally valid for all."[21] Marx counseled followers not to consort with reformist parties or even radical republicans because he believed such reforms were but a trap to soften the resistance of socialist parties. Nevertheless, Marx's activism spanned several decades, and he tempered his views at times, even allowing that in certain advanced countries such as the United States and England, collaboration might be possible. He was, according to Sperber, however, not particularly optimistic. In an exchange with an American journalist, who suggested that English workers had successfully brought about peaceful change, Marx retorted:

> I am not so sanguine on that point as you. The English middle-class has always shown itself willing enough to accept the verdict of the majority so long as it enjoyed the monopoly of the voting power. But mark me, as soon as it finds itself outvoted on what it considers vital questions, we shall see here a new slave-owner's war.[22]

While he did not include terrorism, such as individual assassination, in the war between classes, Marx did think that it was a reasonable strategy in Russia where other forms of action proved impossible.

Yet his endorsement of these tactics did not include Bismarck's Prussia, a quite authoritarian regime.

Violence thus had its place, as Marx often reiterated. Historian David McLellan, in his very helpful analysis, indicated that underlying Marx's insistence on this point was a belief that the proletarian revolution, involving all (or almost all) of society, would be the most radical of all. In this case, it would be not only political but also social and would reach the "point that all class antagonisms were sharpened and simplified to an extent that permitted abolition" of the bourgeoisie.[23] Robert Tucker further explained that at this point Marx thought that the goals of the bourgeoisie and the proletariat could not be reconciled. The former might compromise, providing better distribution of goods and even some power, but this was not the point of the Communist revolution which wanted to end "alienation" or, in other terms, bring about a new redistribution of the fruits of labor. All products would be equally shared. Why? Because Marx envisioned the end of redistribution to be a point in economic evolution when machines did most of the work and people could be freed to spend most of their time as they wished. Man would be emancipated.[24] Tucker assumed but did not directly state that redistribution could not approach the benefits of communism to the proletariat that Marx anticipated. In sum, these analyses explain clearly why Marx was so committed to violent revolution. Although he certainly opined that each stage consisted of a dramatic revolution, the social inclusiveness of the final stage—its appeal—was also so threatening that violent conflict with the new dispossessed (the bourgeoisie) was inevitable.

Other concerns about his theory were also raised during Marx's lifetime. Marx generally articulated his theory in the 1840s, but it gained more followers and detractors in later decades, so it is not surprising that events posed issues for him and Engels. In those halcyon days of nationalism, the map of central Europe was being completely reshaped through Austria's loss of territory and the emergence of Germany (with Prussia as a base) and Italy. Replacing a decentralized empire created two large nation-states, one of which (Germany) was then the most potent economic engine in the world. And workers' parties generally followed national loyalties. What implication would this have on the concept that the revolution would come when the bourgeois states and the forces of capitalism had outlived their productive uses? Marx made strategic compromises with nationalism at times. While allowing that the time for revolution might be ripe in one country or that capitalism might be particularly weak in another, permitting the revolution to begin one place or another, Marx avowed that this spark of revolution might engender international uprisings. Here he used the term "Permanent Revolution," which the Bolsheviks later adopted. Thus, for revolution to succeed, even while it might have begun in one region, the overall readiness of the capitalist system to collapse would be necessary. Another related question that later became very relevant to the Bolsheviks was whether a stage in economic development could be skipped in an individual country. Marx seems to have answered affirmatively but believed such could occur only with assistance from international forces. Marx even declared that the peasantry might start a revolution but it would be only a "fulcrum" for the "social regeneration" of Russia in general and could occur only if the proletarians there had already grown in class consciousness.[25] But that revolution too could only survive by gaining assistance from other revolutions where conditions had fully ripened.

This discussion would have implications for how Communist theory on sovereignty evolved. All the way back to the *Communist Manifesto*, Marx called for "workers of the world to unite" to make a revolution; yet by the late nineteenth century, he imagined the workers might seize power in one state in order to propagate communism into a world order. Thus even in his lifetime, ambiguity emerged about the requirements for seizing authority. The Russians made a revolution in expectation of outside help, but later had to accept they had made an isolated revolution with a willingness to engage a community of communist countries, even if only in the remote future. Other later insurrections ended up following the Russian model from the start—that is making national communist states. Later on, the notion of "proletariat" would also change.

Marx and Engels were exceptionally laconic on the specific contours of the communist era. Over time, when explaining how the revolution would implement a new communist society and economy, Marx advanced the notion that the "dictatorship of the proletariat" would be brief and would provide the means to usher in the new social relations. Famously, he noted that then the state "would wither away." As he clarified this concept, he noted that political power would evaporate, but administrative units would continue to exist. Society might be said to have ended "alienation" in the economic realm when only one social class existed. This, he noted, would evolve over time with the experience of this new society. In this system where all people worked, they could likely work fewer hours. While fixed human desires would also continue, they would be ameliorated by the end of class domination. As noted above, machines would provide a higher standard of living, including more free time. At their most optimistic, Marx and Engels predicted the end of the alienating division of labor:

> In communist society, where nobody has one exclusive sphere of activity but each can become accomplished in any branch he wishes, society regulates the general production and thus makes it possible for me to do one thing today and another tomorrow, to hunt in the morning, fish in the afternoon, rear cattle in the evening, criticise after dinner, just as I have in mind, without ever becoming hunter, fisherman, shepherd or critic. This fixation of social activity, this consolidation of what we ourselves produce into an objective power above us, growing out of our control, thwarting our expectations, bringing to naught our calculations, is one of the chief factors in historical development up till now.[26]

Here they seemed to echo Fourier, and to a certain extent the happiness promised by the American and French revolutions, in a manner consistent with Tucker's interpretation that Marx expected man to be set free.

Future Marxist revolutionaries would gain advantage over competitors from the projection of this future—whether it included unlimited freedom or the more modest claim in the Communist Manifesto that economic resources would be equitably divided. In fact, such projections justified the Party's drive for sovereignty on behalf of the "masses." Even when the reality did not presently match up to expectations, Marx's "scientific" history of class struggle also promised that the ultimate goal would be reached. Thus, using the Marxist label could justify both seizure of power and current privations.

Finally, no description of Marx would be complete without discussing his form of presenting and emphasizing his opinions. Although Marx wrote as both theorist and as a polemicist, it was in this latter mode that he reached his contemporaries. Most scholars agree that his two most effective, even lyrical works, the *Communist Manifesto* and *The Eighteenth Brumaire of Louis Bonaparte*, constituted the outer parameter of his skill. The essay accompanying this chapter suggests that Marx's style matched well the fictional modes of the age, adding appeal to his message. Still, at his death, Marx could not claim any significant progress for his ideas. He well might have been appalled or delighted by their later reception.

Nevertheless, he might have taken pride that he had unconsciously addressed an issue that confounded early revolutionaries in the United States, France, and Latin America. Marx's own "utopian" economic and social solution directly dealt with the problem that Babeuf confronted: creating a strong government necessary to run a country with the rights and privileges due equal men, creations of God. For Marx, industrial success would provide so much wealth that humans could do as they wished, the state withering away and replaced by an administration, seemingly functioning as no more than a traffic light. Perhaps nationalists might envision that their ideology would reduce bickering and create a society/state equilibrium, whose motives were properly aligned. Later Marxist and Islamic revolutionaries, as discussed below, also provided their solutions to this conundrum. But where nationalists had brought a new emphasis on cultural particularities or ethnicity or distinctive social histories to the meaning of revolution, Marx and Engels added a powerful new insistence on the centrality of economic forces and economic conflicts in *all* revolutionary upheavals. After Marx, revolution increasingly meant economic transformation even more than the late eighteenth-century claims for human rights. And in the process of considering and applying Marxist thought to contemporary issues, Marx, Engels, and others debated and created adaptations to these basic theoretical questions, some of which can be considered in the next chapters.

Should Marx be considered an heir to the French Revolution?

Essay 2

Marx on the Pulpit

A deeper understanding of Karl Marx, the activist, should consider his polemical style, a subject that compared with his ideas, his political involvement, and his biography has been too little examined by historians. To provide context and contrast, it is useful to relate his approach with that of his contemporary Alexis de Tocqueville, a classical liberal.

Scholars have identified Marx's *The Eighteenth Brumaire of Louis Bonaparte* as one of his most creative and scintillating works. At its publication in 1851, Tocqueville had already authored his still-famous *Democracy in America* and would produce his heralded *The Old Regime and the French Revolution* as well as a journal about the revolution of 1848. Many scholars consider his book on the French Revolution, although he had only completed the part to 1789, as the most important work on the subject.

Given their dissimilar political outlooks, Marx and Tocqueville interpreted quite differently the Revolution of 1848 which not only shook France but also created shock waves very broadly in Europe. In France the event occurred as a wide body of progressives revolted in 1848 against King Louis-Philippe, whose regime had become dominated by the interests of the wealthy. A series of convulsions followed, including most notably, a very ambitious progressive government that created a system of "workshops" for the unemployed; a major revolt in Paris in June 1848 to protest the closing of the "workshops," followed by the election of a conservative legislature; and the subsequent election of Louis Bonaparte, Napoleon I's nephew, as president in December 1848 and his successful coups to become first president for life in 1851, and then Emperor in 1852.

Marx, not surprisingly, found even the early, most aggressive phases of this new revolution insufficiently radical. Already in 1848, he had published the *Communist Manifesto*, which has also been praised for its clarity and stylistic accomplishments. For the newspaper, the *Neue Rheinische Zeitung*, written in Cologne and then London, Marx penned a series of articles, published in a book form in 1850 as *Class Struggle in France, 1848–1850.*[27] He produced a different version of these events, *The Eighteenth Brumaire of Louis Bonaparte* that finished the tale and appeared in 1853.[28]

Although Tocqueville also wrote about and participated extensively in the Revolution of 1848, his background and career differed enormously from Marx. Born into an important noble lineage in 1805, Alexis de Tocqueville gained fame as a traveler in the United States who presented his ruminations about that society in *Democracy in America* (1835), still read by students of American history and politics. Throughout his public life, he embraced democracy, believed in the importance of property, and opposed governmental centralization. Nonetheless, in 1848 he found himself supporting a state-imposed solution as the only way to ensure property rights and public order. With such views he held a governmental position, even during Louis Napoleon's presidency, but could not tolerate the coup d'état in 1851. However, *Recollections*, his journal published posthumously in 1893, had been written during the events of 1848–1849.[29]

Selections from Marx's work and Tocqueville's journal provide cameos of each man's ideology as well as showing their stylistic and rhetorical differences. Marx's introduction outlined his overall understanding, which he then supplemented with a long analysis of the June Days (1848), the most violent period of that revolution in France.

Marx's title presaged his overall perspective. The eighteenth of Brumaire (November 9, 1799) was the date on the revolutionary calendar when Napoleon I participated in a coup that soon catapulted him to be the leader of France. Marx clearly meant his title to be provocative and to attack the legitimacy of Louis-Napoleon's office by associating him with the previous coup by his famous ancestor. Any possibility that Marx would be even handed disappeared in his first sentence.

My focus is more on Marx's mode of attack than its substance. Marx began this book with a line so poignant that it has been frequently quoted: "Hegel remarks somewhere that all facts and personages of great importance in world history occur, as it were, twice. He forgot to add: the first time as tragedy, the second as farce."[30] Marx then continued with various examples of the second act: Luther as Paul; the French Revolutionaries as Romans; and the revolutions of 1848 as various parts of the French Revolution of 1789. Arguing that the people performed heroic tasks in 1848, Marx also believed that they then found themselves buried under the ghosts of former revolutions, including the "adventurer [Louis-Napoleon], who hides his common repulsive features under the iron death mask of Napoleon [I]."[31] In fact, contemporaries, including Louis Napoleon's wife, found him unsightly. Not only did Marx invoke appearance, but he also referred to the lost freedom and new tax burdens and directly blamed the French people. At the election that Louis-Napoleon had won in 1848, the French thought they were getting Napoleon I and indeed they did. Marx grimly added that the Napoleon I they obtained was not the emperor at the height of powers but only a later caricature of him.

Having compared the current government to a standard, which it could never attain in the memories of the French and even the Europeans, Marx then provided a commentary on the three years since the onset of the Revolution of 1848. At its beginning in February 1848, the revolutionary uprising took the old society by surprise, and the "people" proclaimed a new epoch. Yet when the constitution was announced in December 1848, "what seems overthrown is no longer the monarchy but the liberal concessions that were wrung from it by centuries of struggle," when nobles and prelates had been in charge. "Easy come, easy go," commented Marx, arguing that the French had fallen back with fewer rights than before.[32]

He then supplied the revolution's epitaph.

> The Constitution, the National Assembly, the dynastic parties, the blue and the red republicans, the heroes of Africa, the thunder from the platform, the sheet lightning of the daily press, the entire literature, the political names and the intellectual reputations, the civil law and the penal code, the *liberté, égalité, fraternité* and the second Sunday in May 1852—all has vanished like a phantasmagoria before the spell of a man whom even his enemies do not make out to be sorcerer. Universal suffrage seems to have survived only for a

> moment, in order that with its own hand it may make its last will and testament before the eyes of all the world and declare in the name of the people itself: All that exists deserves to perish.[33]

This devastating dismissal of the Revolution of 1848 used history, irony, sarcasm, and graceful turns of phrase. Disappearing in a puff, the revolution, in Marx's characterization, was a comedic repetition of history. More important, Marx vehemently indicted even the populace who had been hoodwinked by the banal Louis-Napoleon. In the remainder of his pamphlet, Marx denounced the bourgeoisie as corrupt, pusillanimous, and weak. In short, he undertook no fair-minded judicious analysis but instead mounted a brutal and devastating attack on French society. The hostility and radicalism he showed toward the failure of the French is important, but the power and sharp blows of his prose should not be discounted.

And in fact, Tocqueville also bitterly criticized the politicians who aided and abetted the failures of the revolution. His cynicism, more guarded to be sure, was effective through snide insinuations as well as direct attacks. His charges against politicians generally were personal, rather than ideological. Overall, his most important point was that the mediocre record of the Revolution of 1848 was the best outcome to avert the disaster that would have occurred had the popular revolution triumphed. Like Marx, he believed that a more radical revolution had been blocked; unlike Marx, however, he believed this failure was essential for France.

From the beginning of his account, Tocqueville showed a ferocious, out-of-control laboring class. During the June days of the popular uprising in 1848, he described the masses—using geological, geographical, and hygienic metaphors—to indicate the threat they posed. At first Tocqueville more charitably portrayed the efforts of the workers to escape their poverty. Misled by others, they assumed that their poverty had been caused by the thievery of the comfortable.[34]

Tocqueville's description took a more sinister cast when the radicals fighting in the streets seemed to be threatening the whole social order—with which he clearly identified. He called the insurrection terrible, inspired by cupidity.[35] And he saw a battle everywhere: "Even the places where we thought we were masters were creeping with domestic enemies ...." As actual fighting began, he found the noise emanating from the districts "a diabolical music, a mixture of drums and trumpets, whose offensive, discordant savage sounds were new to me." Everywhere he saw workers with "sinister expressions." An old woman had a "frightful and hideous expression ... reflect[ing] demagogic passions and the fury of evil." These references to the massed workers suggested how they seemed more and problematic. At first this body was strong and encompassing.[36] As it gained ground, ominously like a cloud "it stretched as long as far out into the suburbs."[37]

Tocqueville related two connected anecdotes about domestic servants that also more fully communicated his viewpoint. The first concerned the author's own doorkeeper who, after the revolt's initial success told his barroom pals that he intended to kill Tocqueville and showed the knife with which he intended to do the deed. Upon learning of the boast, Tocqueville decided he would not return home but knew of nowhere else to go. There he found the doorman. The two jockeyed for position as they walked to Tocqueville's door, with the doorman mainly in front, thus forfeiting the element of surprise. Arriving at the door, Tocqueville entered, and only then did the doorman follow the usual courtesy and take off his hat and bow. The entire episode conveyed the intended victim's dangerous position.

Contrast that account of the potentially violent doorman with the arrival of Tocqueville's manservant the next day. Waking in a start at the sound of a key in the lock, the gentleman found that his valet, "that fine fellow," had left his post with the National Guard, in order to clean Tocqueville's boots, brush his clothes, and generally to tend to domestic duties. No socialist in theory or inclination, the valet was untouched "by that most unusual sickness of our time, a restless mind ...." He remained pleased with himself and others. "... he generally desired nothing beyond his reach ...." His balance brought his happiness. And he reassured Tocqueville that, despite the echoes of gunfire, things were going well and "will end very well." Having completed his duties, the valet announced that he would return to battle. For the next four days he went back and forth between house and post as the fighting continued. "In those troubled days of savagery and hatred, it gave me a sense of repose to see that young man's peaceful, satisfied face."[38]

No two accounts of the 1848 revolution in Paris could differ more than Marx's and Tocqueville's, and they provide an excellent contrast. The revolution unfortunately failed because a charlatan had betrayed the people; the revolution was sinister, but fortunately good men opposed it. The divide between the two sides was cavernous.

Likewise, the rhetorical distance was vast. Analyzing two political books to determine their rhetorical style as well as their explicit meaning is necessarily speculative. But Marx's opinions were marked, clear, and aggressive. Tocqueville's themes used metaphors and anecdotes to reach the opposite side of the analytical, political spectrum. Marx depicted his enemies as lying and prevaricating; Tocqueville saw the people's feints, sinister grins, and distant gunfire. In Tocqueville's view, the doorman proved weak and vacillating; his boasts were shallow and evanescent. Indeed, Tocqueville portrayed the masses as sinister but also insubstantial like a cloud. Marx matched well the passions of a tragic, romantic novel; Tocqueville, like a latter-day Montesquieu, employed the reticent analytical fictional style of the Enlightenment that had to maneuver its way through censorship. Mid-nineteenth-century European revolutionaries found Marx's style more appealing and convincing. Violent revolution had produced its most visible and consistent advocate. And while many feared his ideas, Marx became the secular prophet with the widest reach. And Tocqueville's pettiness, no doubt, would have cost him support among those whom he might have tried to convince. The doorman was castigated for a lack of courtesy; the valet praised for his obsequious obedience. Clearly, Tocqueville's expectations of subservience showed him to be a man of the past for whom social change was not in the future.

What does Marx share with Paine? How are the two different? Answer the same questions for Burke and Tocqueville?

Further Reading

Adelman, Jeremy. *Sovereignty and Revolution in the Iberian Atlantic*. Princeton, 2006.

Bell, David A. *The Cult of the Nation in France: Inventing Nationalism, 1680–1800*. Cambridge, MA, 2001.

Billington, James H. *Fire in the Minds of Men: Origins of the Revolutionary Faith*. New York, 1980.

Chasteen, John Charles. *Americanos: Latin America's Struggle for Independence*. New York, 2008.

Eisenstein, Elizabeth L. *The First Professional Revolutionist: Filippo Michele Buonarroti, 1761–1837: A Biographical Essay*. Cambridge, MA, 1959.

Kramer, Lloyd. *Nationalism in Europe & America: Politics, Cultures, and Identities since 1775*. Chapel Hill, 2011.

Lasso, Marixa. *Myths of Harmony: Race and Republicanism during the Age of Revolution, 1795–1831*. Pittsburgh, 2007.

Manuel, Frank E. *The Prophets of Paris: Turgot, Condorcet, Saint-Simon, Fourier, and Comte*. Cambridge, MA, 1962.

Patriarca, Silvana and Lucy Riall. Ed. *The Risorgimento Revisited: Nationalism and Culture in Nineteenth-Century*. New York, 2012.

Riall, Lucy. *Garibaldi: Invention of a Hero*. New Haven and London, 2007.

Riall, Lucy. *The Italian Risorgimento: State, Society and National Unification*. London and New York, 1994.

Rose, R.B. *Gracchus Babeuf: The First Revolutionary Communist*. Stanford, 1978.

Smith, Denis Mack. *Mazzini*. New Haven and London, 1994.

Sperber, Jonathan. *Karl Marx: A Nineteenth-Century Life*. New York, 2013.

Tucker, Robert C. *The Marxian Revolutionary Idea*. New York, 1969.

Van Young, Eric. *The Other Rebellion: Popular Violence, Ideology, and the Mexican Struggle for Independence, 1810–1821*. Stanford, 2001.

3

Communism and the Modern Social Meaning of Revolutions Led by Centralized Parties, 1880–1949

Everybody knows that Russia and China experienced communist revolutions, but explaining what these ruptures entailed is not so simple. In the most elemental sense, those who made these revolutions believed that Marx had laid out the best pattern for liberating humanity. These enormous revolutions are linked by their size, vast importance, and the former's influence on the latter, not because the revolutionaries completely agreed on policy, but because they and contemporaries saw important linkages to the theories espoused by Marx and each other.

Marx tended at times to describe communism as more thorough going than socialism and thus denoted it as more radical. Bolshevik revolutionaries embraced the strong term early in the revolution. The name stuck: like the Russians, the more self-consciously radical of later times, including the Chinese, called themselves communists, while others were socialists or social democrats. Over time, these latter terms were applied to thoroughly nonrevolutionary parties.

This chapter explores the two greatest and most cataclysmic communist revolutions to comprehend how each developed ideologically. Vladimir Ilyich Lenin was unquestionably the most influential of the Russian leaders; understanding his ideas, which informed the movement, requires beginning with the beliefs that first influenced him and continuing past his lifetime to examine how his successors interpreted and utilized his views. The second half of this chapter explains the ideological lineage of the Chinese revolutionaries.

Previous revolutionary ideas like democracy and freedom continued but communism evolved new concepts that inspired many twentieth-century revolutionaries. And, in fact, the communist revolutions proved preeminent in establishing new models for progressive-minded violent revolutions. Nationalism had also inspired revolution, but the victors of the First World War gave the greatest impetus to creating nation-based governments by rewriting the world map according to that goal immediately after 1918. This nation-building was disrupting, but it appeared then to be a simple, more peaceful imposition of change than had recently been spreading throughout the world by war and conflagration. So it is communism, which in some countries, including China, also had strongly nationalistic as well as cosmopolitan or internationalist dimensions, that must draw our attention.

During the Cold War, many scholars suggested that communist flexibility showed a corrosive self-interest and indicted these revolutionaries. Recent scholarship, however, suggests that such ideological changes mainly resulted from the efforts required and the commitment to bring such principles into reality. But as in the case of the Jacobins, much violence, a horrific death toll, and international interference accompanied these passionate beliefs. This work mainly focuses on ideas and their development.

The Russian Revolution

Although at his death on May 30, 1918 (from natural causes), Georgi Plekhanov was not in favor with the communist revolutionaries who had seized power the preceding autumn, he received full honors and the appellation, "Father of Russian Marxism." In fact, as one of the first Russian adherents to socialism, Plekhanov had towered over Lenin before the latter's ascendance in the Russian party at the turn of the twentieth century. Though rivals, they had remained on good terms up to the First World War. Thus, any account of the Russian revolutionary idea should begin with Plekhanov.

Born into a noble family in 1856, Plekhanov seems to have experienced no seminal event that launched him into revolutionary activity. As a student in his early twenties in St. Petersburg, he apparently was influenced by the desire for change in those circles and started his career as an agrarian populist.

Although French Revolutionary ideas at first had less impact on Russia than in Western Europe, the 1860s witnessed a significant stirring. Among the numerous competing concepts was a violent anarchism which felled several officials, including even one of the tsars. Plekhanov was first intrigued by the populist Narodniks who encouraged the recently freed serfs (emancipated in 1861) to seize all the land and administer it through community rule. After this movement failed dramatically, Plekhanov drifted toward the more terroristic causes but was hesitant about movements where the revolutionary ardor seemed to eclipse serious commitment to substantive political change. Most important, after his activities landed him in trouble with the authorities, he fled to Switzerland where he encountered Marxists as well as an entire panoply of revolutionary movements.

During the 1890s, Plekhanov became a disciple of orthodox Marxist thought, varying little from the general direction outlined by Marx himself in the *Communist Manifesto*. Russia's intense underdevelopment made adapting Marxist theory difficult. But to Plekhanov and many others, the signs of industrial growth in Russia made Marx's theory more appealing than agrarian populism which had so disappointed. Because Russia had not even reached the stage of bourgeois domination, Plekhanov had to design a Marxism that could convince others to join a party whose first task was empowering wealthy commoners to overthrow autocracy. Engels had already noted that launching such an effort would not be incorrect. In fact, Plekhanov argued that as the socialists and the proletariat worked first to empower the bourgeoisie, they would at the same time be establishing a workers' party that could accelerate a later transition to social democracy.

Like Marx, Plekhanov was striving to balance his clear acceptance of the stages of revolution with calls to action in Russia, accepting even the "dictatorship of the proletariat," a transitional stage run by the triumphant working class and mentioned in the *Communist Manifesto*. Possibly more important, Plekhanov began to outline another concept that would become extremely important in future Russian thought. Perhaps, he hypothesized, Russia's capitalist phase might be further shortened by international intervention, led by a regime that had already achieved a socialist revolution elsewhere. Marx himself was friendly to this kind of revision. Or possibly, inspired by socialist victories abroad, the Russian proletariat might leap into the breach, expecting assistance from another country. Such approaches did not undermine the overall economic determinism as the general situation was, in fact, "ready" to go. Such tension among those inspired by the *Communist Manifesto*, while completely understandable in a group trying to build a party, did open the door to innovative theories of Marxian development. Indeed, as noted above, Marx had, in his vast correspondence, stated that such variations were possible.

While no particularly traumatic event, other than his flight from Russia to avoid prosecution, led Plekhanov to radicalism, or even to Marxism, Lenin left Russia after a much more problematic chain of circumstances. His older brother Alexander, as a student in St. Petersburg, had become involved in radical politics in 1886. First he joined protests against Tsar Alexander III whose father, Alexander II, had been assassinated in 1881. More student than revolutionary, Alexander Ulyanov participated in a bombing plot to kill the monarch. Although he was not one of the bombers, Alexander was arrested for his involvement and soon executed. This event had a profound impact on Vladimir who, in a society that believed in collective guilt, was removed from school and the comfortable life of his own bourgeois family. Not only the authorities, but polite society also persecuted the family. In fact, according to one of the many Lenin biographers, Bertram D. Wolfe, the hostility of his own social class wounded Lenin most deeply and created in him an uncompromising hostility to the middle classes.[1] This hatred of the bourgeoisie contrasted with his empathy for the widow of Alexander II. Although, noted Lenin, the assassination was good for Russia, he could grieve with the widow. Temperamentally, Lenin worked from a different wellspring of anger than Plekhanov.

Drawn into politics while continuing his schooling, Lenin more and more played an active role in association with Russian Marxists. He had already begun to encounter Marxist writings including those by Plekhanov; for the next decade, he kept generally in step with Plekhanov. Lenin also remained very active both in political agitation and in meeting others prominent in the movement. After arrest and a three-year sentence to Siberia, Lenin finally emigrated, spending almost two decades outside of Russia.

Shortly after his arrival abroad, Lenin joined the leadership group of the Russian Social Democrats and began to make a reputation, especially with what proved to be his most influential work, *What Is to Be Done?*, published in 1902.[2] This book was Lenin's first attempt to adapt Marxist theory to his view of the situation in Russia. In short, he believed that the intelligentsia would constitute the leadership of the party and would include a powerful centralized leadership. As noted in the previous chapter, the *Communist Manifesto* had certainly included the party in the plans for a revolution, but Marx had imagined its most forward role to be educating the masses as activists sought to raise their consciousness. The workers would seize power and would wield the "dictatorship" of the proletariat themselves. Lenin's innovation can be interpreted as only a friendly amendment, but as explored in this chapter and its essay, his vision of the relationship between workers and party leadership differed sharply in tone as well as in specific aspects with Marx's seminal work. And it was also a battle to justify seizing power and changing the terms of sovereignty, not a workers' onslaught but a disciplined party acting with the workers to create a revolution. But in this tract and throughout the drive to power, the party should lead even as some workers were to be recruited to the party. Some scholars have described Lenin's change as moving from a dictatorship of the proletariat to a dictatorship of a centralized party.

Other historians believe that Marx would have been amenable to many of these changes as the failure of the revolutions of 1848–1849 had made him embrace the possibility of secret, conspiratorial parties. And still other scholars argue that in fact Lenin meant to fuse the party as much as possible to the workers and thus virtually fulfill Marx's notion of a proletariat leading the revolution. Such debates will not die because they are so important to evaluating the entire communist experience. But they provide a good corrective to previous scholarship designed to prosecute the Party as mainly selfish in its aims.

What circumstances led Lenin to produce this pamphlet and adopt this notion of sovereignty? His prior personal involvement in conspiracies and a drive to effect change possibly made him open to doctrinal alterations that would accelerate matters rather simply anticipate the slow "maturation" of the proletariat. He was also affected by the specific circumstances of late nineteenth-century Europe. When Marx had first studied Western societies and economies and co-authored the *Communist Manifesto*, the modern industrial working class was just emerging. Outside England, large factories were scarce and only beginning to replace artisanal production. Though Marx had correctly forecast the growth of industry, in fact revolutionary parties continued to debate and failed to capitalize on the expansion of industry. For his intellectual descendants, this proved problematic. The theory needed updating to provide more direct action. Moreover, most Marxists had embraced the theory as a validated, data-driven plan to achieve the moral good of socialism which generally promised both equality and freedom. Theoretical correction thus seemed necessary to achieve the moral goal. As noted, Marx himself was more than open to changes, particularly those more likely to produce revolution.

Prominent were the various nonrevolutionary versions of Marxism then emerging. Some party members expounded "legal Marxism" which in Russia relied on legally publishable materials. Carefully constructed to pass censorship, these intellectuals' works affirmed revolutionary goals. Published abroad, journals such as *The Worker's Cause* also undermined radicalism by emphasizing action to achieve economic goals such as state regulation of working conditions, social security measures, child labor prohibitions, and the like. While this group still believed in the eventual triumph of socialism, its members were willing to settle for intermediate measures. Finally, and these various views mingled, some revisionists believed that "free" countries would eventually see the triumph of socialism through the vote. Even Marx, toward the end of his life, imagined some countries achieving socialism through parliamentary action, though he was generally skeptical. Marx thought a lot, wrote a lot, and proved enormously inconsistent, except about achieving socialism as the end game.

Lenin generally rejected such a revision of Marx's original beliefs in the inevitable violent march to socialism and insisted that revolutionary goals should be achieved through a directed party linked to workers. Here he was reacting to the particular Russian conditions in his country, which was authoritarian and agricultural, though industry was advancing. Also stimulating his more aggressive stand may have been the halting advance of parliamentary democracy when compared with most other Western nations. Thus, he began a discussion about sovereignty. The Party would be a well-honed tool designed to drive change. For many twenty-first-century readers, political warfare over intellectual nuances might seem difficult to understand, but these writers and activists firmly believed that doctrine and ideas were the route to communism and the stakes were immense. In fact, the failure of the tsarist regimes to open society to electoral politics and legitimate parliaments provided the backdrop for the nature of this battle. Instead of practicing normal politics, Lenin agitated for radical change against those inclined to await further social evolution. The outcome of this internecine squabble over strategic tactics—Lenin's victory—would have a great impact on world history during the following decades.

Lenin's continued call for a centralized party preceded a congress of socialists held in Brussels in the summer of 1903. A rancorous debate over party centralization erupted there and led to the dominance for Lenin's role of the party. Although Plekhanov and Lenin had expressed different views on this subject, they united at this time. Lenin determinedly pushed forward his notion of a party composed of professional revolutionaries that, with some members of the working class integrated into the Party, would provide leadership to the working class as a whole. Highly motivated workers could, it became clear later, be trained to enter the core. This would be the best way to hasten the revolution. His opponents wanted a less conspiratorial party. At the first vote, Lenin seemed to be losing, but in the end he won. A walkout by several moderate delegates allowed Lenin to snatch victory. In a brilliant linguistic stroke, he called his faction the Bolsheviks, the Russian word for "majority," and the defeated group "the Mensheviks" (the minority). Although subsequent scholars tended to reify the differences, the two sides mainly worked together over time with different views competing.

After this battle, the party faced another crisis in 1905, after the Russians launched an aggressive war in 1904 against the Japanese. Expecting to defeat easily an Asian nation, Russia experienced humiliating defeat after defeat. Under enormous pressure from a broad ideological spectrum including supporters of the monarchy, Nicholas II's government responded by attacking St. Petersburg workers who mounted a series of marches to push for political rights, workplace improvements, and better living conditions. Troops used gunfire to disperse the crowd and killed hundreds of protesters. A broad-based popular revolutionary effort followed, without significant Marxist input. Roundly criticized, facing massive strikes, and realizing the poor reputation of the monarchy, the demoralized government issued a manifesto that *de jure* made Russia a constitutional monarchy. Had history turned out differently, these events could have been "the" Russian Revolution, but subsequent occurrences made 1905 only a prelude to 1917.

Royal disaster created both opportunity for and consternation among the socialist movement that earlier had seen uncertain prospects. In particular, Leon Trotsky, a younger member of the party without strong allegiances in it, proposed a major challenge to earlier tactics. Witnessing the power of resistance that emerged throughout Russia during the Russo-Japanese War, he imagined that a partnership of peasants and workers could compensate for Russia's backwardness and through continuous effort, which he called "permanent revolution," lead to a socialist takeover. Marx had used the term "permanent revolution" to describe a worker's revolution that would spread from one country to another. Trotsky's proposal, another variation on the right to claim sovereignty, promised to expand the social base that the party might represent. His proposal questioned two very important positions that most Marxists had expounded and still believed. First, Trotsky argued that the peasants could be more than a mere reactionary force. Just as important,

Russia might not need international help but instead could muster enough power itself to create a successful revolution. In other words, the revolution might be sparked in a more agrarian society, weak in economic development, rather than in a mature capitalist country. Lenin was interested but not convinced; others were opposed, but these innovations could not go further at the time. After 1905, the monarchy stabilized and regained the political influence lost during the war; the economy strengthened; and the revolutionary option receded. By 1912, Lenin believed that further revolutionary opportunity was far away.

Then the First World War changed everything. Like many countries, Russia began the war in 1914 with significant optimism and support. But soon, the underindustrialized country could not compete with the Germans, and Russian troops experienced terrible privations and military defeats. In February 1917, an unplanned popular uprising, started by workers and then joined by the general urban population and finally by the Petrograd (modern-day St. Petersburg) garrison, overthrew Nicholas II who quickly departed. Distracted by his hemophilic son and his difficult wife, he was advised to abdicate, but no suitable replacement as tsar could be found. Replacing him was a republican provisional government soon to be led by Alexander Kerensky, at most a moderate socialist and certainly no Bolshevik. A liberal, Menshevik, and Socialist Revolutionary coalition maintained a fragile balance of power. Its socialist members saw it as achieving the bourgeois stage, necessary before the takeover by socialists.

In April, Lenin, upon his German-assisted return from Switzerland where he had spent the war, pushed the Bolsheviks to take more aggressive action to push the Petrograd Soviet (a spontaneously created worker council like those in other large cities) and the Provisional Government toward sweeping revolution. He asserted that the bourgeois stage had matured and the time had arrived for the revolution. Some colleagues did not find this evident, and it seemed an enormous departure from the widely held notion that communism could only seize power after bourgeois society had much further matured. But others concurred. Lenin, with his indomitable will, soon won the day. What actually happened? Post–Cold War historians have argued that Lenin, presented with a revolution, believed it a chance to institute socialism, while previously many scholars had simply interpreted it as a power grab. Recently, Andrez Mun Walichi asserted that Lenin thought that the workers had generally achieved the proper level of consciousness and class antagonism, even if the economic realities had not changed.[3] Russia was ready for radical change. The Bolsheviks might seize power in their name.

On another point of doctrine, promulgated during the war, Lenin had already been changing his mind. In his new book on imperialism, Lenin concluded that capitalism was evolving into a global system of monopolies and financial markets that controlled the rest of the world. Producing enormous differences in profits without reference to productive forces, this global financial conflict inevitably led to wars among the capitalists, as the Great War of 1914 seemed clearly to demonstrate. Among the weakest global competitors, Russia was extremely vulnerable to exploitation by others and economic collapse. Such a crisis could make the country the starting point for a socialist revolution.

Lenin's new ideas on imperialism accelerated his inclination toward initiating revolution in Russia. To be sure, all the Bolsheviks believed, much like Marx, despite the continued presence of various notions of permanent revolution, that the action of one isolated, underdeveloped nation to establish socialism required revolutions in the advanced countries of Europe to provide armed support and economic assistance to transform Russia's economy. Given the course of the war and the turbulence among European countries, this, they posited, would be likely to occur. Lenin, asserting that history was on his side, went forward with a strategic revolutionary plan. After some setbacks, in November (Western calendar), the Bolsheviks successfully deposed the initial revolutionary government and took control.

In retrospect, the last advance of the Bolshevik toward a seizure of power may seem inevitable, but events could actually have evolved quite differently. Although a coalition government headed by Alexander Kerensky, a Social Revolutionary whose party was somewhat a descendant of the Narodniks, installed liberalism with democracy, freedom of speech, and the end of police repression, it did not solve the economic or military problems that had so plagued the country during the war. First, Kerensky's plan for land redistribution was not implemented, and despite the dire situation of Russia's military forces (success in fighting the Austrians but utter failure against the Germans), the government supported the war aims of their Western allies and continued to fight. The commitment to democracy also broke down, and the government did not call for a vote to elect a legislature in time to win respect. Against these failures, the Bolsheviks promised land, peace, and worker supervision of industry, a platform that appealed to many. They adopted an appealing slogan of "All Power to the Soviets" which vowed respect for the average person. The Soviets had become extremely popular by 1917, gaining the support of the industrial workers who were growing in size and influence. Linking to these bodies and their enthusiastic support gave the Bolsheviks substantial further credibility to advance against the Provisional Government in fall 1917. Surprisingly and shockingly, having established authority in major cities, the Bolsheviks experienced relatively few casualties until after the initial struggle for power. The new communist government established its authority, and neutralized dissent throughout the country in the weeks following the revolution. Thus, military and political collapse opened the doors to the Bolsheviks who exploited the opportunity to install the revolution they had long planned.

With sovereignty more or less in hand, what precisely would the Bolsheviks do with this power? The exercise of authority in the decade immediately following the takeover cemented the ideas of a party whose doctrine emanating from Marx had recently come to be known as Marxist–Leninist. Three intertwined issues became very important: the interaction between the party and the state; the implementation of socialist policy; and the role of international revolution in the survival of the state.

The first test of Bolshevik political power came at a scheduled meeting of Russia's Constituent Assembly, a national body elected in the previous fall to write a new constitution. Only 170 of the total 707 members in attendance were Bolsheviks. Even divided as they were, a majority were Social Revolutionaries. Troops dispersed this gathering that possibly could have reversed the Bolshevik victory, and Lenin began to take steps to create the dictatorship that he believed necessary to initiate a socialist country. In September, Lenin had already argued that the party would dominate politics and thus take control of the economy. Although the Bolsheviks only fitfully put governmental processes in motion, they quickly controlled the bureaucracy. Press censorship followed, as well as the arrests of former moderates. The Bolsheviks had come to believe that, while keeping a centralized democracy alive in their worker/party coalition, only those allied with and subservient to the Bolsheviks would be courted and could add their views. The Bolsheviks believed the rest likely were enemies, disingenuously using openness to destroy the revolution. And state terror was soon unleashed. By late December of 1917 the government had organized the Cheka (a partial acronym) to suppress counterrevolution and sabotage. At the very beginning of its regime, the Communists thus replaced the Tsarist police with a ruthless force of their own. And all this was intensified by the outbreak of civil war that lasted for at least three years.

The movement toward an assertive party and further away from Marx's ideas about working-class leadership and a withering state should be no surprise. Having seized power in a nation used to authoritarian rule, the Bolsheviks, given the tenuous nature of their grasp on power, must have believed these methods of repression to be key. They also believed that violence, as part of the Marxist revolutionary theory, was necessary and inevitable. Further, the Bolsheviks themselves had endured imprisonment and harassment for years. The Bolshevik leaders had so long worked toward revolution that, just as seizing power seemed inevitable, so was defending it with all necessary force. As Trotsky warned, "You wax indignant at the naked Terror which we are applying against our class enemies, but let me tell you that in one month's time [i.e., January 1, 1918] at the most it will assume more frightful forms, modeled on the terror of the great French revolutionaries. Not the fortress [incarceration] but the guillotine will await our enemies."[4]

Even during the raging civil war, the Bolsheviks began to provide workers a voice in factories and spread education among the lower classes. As the Bolsheviks forcefully imposed their power controlling the state, they also began a project to inject the working classes into leadership in state and industry. Even through the Stalin era, this new elite prospered, and more and more joined the Party and rose to responsible positions. In short, ideology, self-preservation, and a reliance on violence combined while the party sought proletarianization of the new, revolutionary society.

Peasants too experienced monumental change. The Bolsheviks found that by the time they took power, peasants had begun to appropriate the means of production and had seized land for themselves. Beyond this, at a local level, the Bolsheviks supported even more radical action as peasants and others used intimidation and confiscated other property. The Decree on Land confirmed this spontaneous action in the countryside by legalizing these seizures and accelerating such actions. Poorer peasants often received property to equalize holdings in peasant communes. This extraordinary social revolution, whose occurrence can scarcely be imagined in Western Europe and North America without creating an outbreak of vigilantism in defense of property, eventually did threaten the economy. By the end of 1917, the Bolsheviks began to apply centralizing measures, which they had embraced in every other economic area, to create national authority to direct the economy. Lenin pushed for discipline and order. But whether state socialism or popular leveling, this was socialism. In 1918, war and counterrevolution forced a continuation and deepening of these tendencies, and the private industry and trade disappeared. All land was nationalized and peasants were forced to deliver a portion of their produce to the state.

The Bolshevik sovereignty had pointed toward social transformation; for that they turned to foreign assistance. Immediate and very embarrassing was the evident contradiction to the theory that international assistance would justify and save the revolution. Although the Bolsheviks shifted Marx's original order of inevitable historical stages moving from capitalism toward socialism, they continued to rely on the rationale, shared with Marx himself, that assistance from more advanced industrial societies abroad might allow this, and thus rationalize their actions according to theory. Generally, they assumed that the fragile socialism erected would likely receive military defense. At other times, the logic seemed to be that if the Russian economy were amalgamated with the European, the Bolsheviks could claim to have attained the overall preconditions for socialism. In any case, the revolution's progress was at first linked to the readiness of Western countries to stand up for Russia.

The war with Germany immediately tested that theory. The Bolsheviks had campaigned for peace as they wanted neither to capitulate to the German war machine nor to aid Western European capitalism by joining the battle. Settling for an armistice limited opportunity as the international "proletariat" was stirring, and Lenin expected according to theory that an international explosion would rescue the revolution. Uninterested in Russian ideas, the Germans insisted on a peace settlement that would have carved off much of Russia's strongest agricultural and industrial sectors. To counter this, Trotsky proposed the slogan "Neither peace nor war," which he believed would encourage the troops of imperialist armies to desert. Instead Germany swept forward in a mighty flood, annexing much more land. Lenin, totally abandoning the international revolutionary ideal, then sued for peace. He argued that any revolutionary war was doomed to failure and that continuing these battles would be suicide for the regime as the "masses" would simply not respond. Facing opposition from within, Lenin expressed the view that outside socialist support would eventually develop, and he justified his call for major concessions by expediency. In fact, in 1921, as European postwar political turmoil stilled, Lenin very consciously accepted that Soviet Russia would be responsible for its own security until world revolution erupted. He had, however, saved the socialist regime.

Indeed, the notion of a world revolution to ratify communism continued to shape Bolshevik expectations for a number of years. To enhance this process, the Russians founded the Comintern to organize communist parties all over the world. But it too became an arm of Soviet survival. Although individuals worldwide idealistically joined these organizations, which at first were somewhat autonomous, overall policy and leadership decisions by the late 1920s came from Moscow. In the Stalinist era, the Comintern vetted leadership selections and made foreign Communist parties' policies align with Russian foreign policy. Indeed, in the 1920s, the Comintern first sponsored comity with other left-wing groups, then battled them when the geopolitical situation changed. Later in the 1930s, to thwart Hitler's ambitions, the Comintern supported popular front movements of Socialists and Communists, only to shift to the right when such a move seemed to aid Russia. In the United States, the Communists, after collaborating with Norman Thomas of the Socialist Party, backed Franklin Roosevelt for president. Foreign communist parties collapsed in 1939, when the Soviets struck a nonaggression treaty with Hitler, and only marginally recovered in 1940, after joining the battle to stop Germany. In the end, the Russians made their revolution without any aid and deployed the Comintern more to spread revolution into other developing countries than to launch revolutions in highly industrialized countries that could enable Russian socialism. For the most part, the Russians hoped for developed countries to be less hostile or possibly even allies on certain issues.

As the preceding events suggest, the Russian communists grew pessimistic about receiving outside assistance and even about the absolute need to seek communist help to save the regime. They had ended up far from the course articulated in the *Communist Manifesto* and claimed and exercised authority in their own name. Yet the actions of the party and its instrument, the state, continued to advance socialism itself. Some Bolsheviks saw "war communism" as a workable path to socialism, even if driven in significant extent by the necessity of supporting the troops. By 1921, however, complete economic collapse and growing popular discontent forced the Bolsheviks to retreat. Gross production had dropped by a third or more. In particular, the peasants lacked incentives to produce for the market and resented the massive and clumsy intrusion of Bolshevik officials. The proletariat shared that discontent because of material privation. Without assistance from the foreign proletariat, Lenin now embraced an economic retreat, the New Economic Policy (NEP). Markets were reopened, and small private businesses could operate; but the state retained control of banking and large enterprises. The economy soon rebounded. In philosophy, the Bolsheviks viewed these NEP policies as a necessary detour on the road to building socialism. By 1924 and 1925, after the death of Lenin, the economy had regained prewar levels, and they began to retreat from the policies and criticize those benefiting from the NEP. The Bolshevik leaders engaged in debate over how and when to abandon NEP and resume the march toward socialism, part of a large struggle over the leadership succession.

Confirming the strength of this intention was Stalin's initiative, as he consolidated power, to institute a "Five-Year Plan" that would in fact create that socialism which was, in the view of the Bolsheviks, the end goal. Peasants were prospering, but not industry and the proletariat, which had from Marx forward, been viewed as the core of socialism. In fact, rank and file communists saw the petty capitalism in cities, the presence of rich peasants, and the seeming abundance of building societies to be a problem. The plan, which transformed Russia into a semi-industrial power, clearly intended to create socialism. It could not change the fact that socialism had not directly emerged from an international revolution, but it promised goals and an era of progress to make Bolsheviks proud. The Five-Year Plan clearly resulted from heavy-handed repressive state imposition, not from a spontaneous revolution. The discomfort with peasant prosperity and comfortable farmers led to a crackdown and the deaths of millions.

Thus was created the first avowedly communist country, but the Marxist ideas inspiring it had been reshaped to include a centralized, dominant party and to bypass the stages of economic development and political actions which the *Communist Manifesto* had propagated. Lenin's own version and specific plans for making a socialist revolution in a backward country did not produce a socialist utopia. Nonetheless, the Bolsheviks had produced a socialist economic and social system. By constructing a tight, centralized party, the Bolsheviks could promote their goals, shift gears, retell the story, behave recklessly when they wished, and force the country down the desired path. The leadership also could keep and expand personal gains. Although Stalin was a product of the system, his personal quirks, perhaps paranoia as many have argued, and the dire international situation exacerbated the worst tendencies of the regime. Like all prior revolutions, this one's costs must be calculated against its gains. Freedoms were limited and as noted, the death toll from various factors was staggering. Yet the Communist state produced the economic power to allow the Soviet Union to beat back Hitler's invasion, win the Second World War in Europe, and prosper significantly from the 1950s into the 1980s. By 1989, many Russians had clearly thought negatively about the revolution, but when they reached that opinion remains a question difficult to answer because those in power were so long unwilling to ask it.

Furthermore, the example of the Russian revolution, a revolution started and continued in one country, set a pattern for others, as communist revolutions proceeded along nationalist lines. The expectation of cordial relations among similar regimes was begun by the Comintern. These various revolutions constituted something of a bloc but generally acted as independent nations.

Debate yourself: Lenin was an opportunist and Lenin was principled.

China

The map of successful revolutions had in fact expanded geographically as such efforts, taking very different forms, marched across the Western world from North America, through Western and Central Europe. By including the Russian Empire in 1917, the phenomenon extended from its roots through Asia, ending at the Pacific shore. The Chinese revolution extended the geographic reach as well as the ideological breadth of modern revolutions. Although the Chinese communist revolution might appear to be simply the application of Western notions of liberty, nationalism, and communism, the Chinese already had a nationalist consciousness long before they had a nationalist government. Further, the nation did not coalesce around Western ideas of socialism as it too improvised Marxist theory.

To understand the Chinese revolution requires a brief review of the state of mid-eighteenth-century Chinese politics and its transformation over the next century. Most scholars contend that under the foreign Manchu rulers the Chinese developed the notion of an ethnicity that should have a unified political regime. Although the Manchus could claim not to be foreign, as during the Taiping rebellion, the Chinese political elite commonly labeled them barbarians. Nonetheless, the Manchus adopted many of the practices of the previous Han dynasty (Ming, 1366–1644) by conserving an elite constituted by its Confucian knowledge and keeping social and gender hierarchies intact. In fact, the Manchu dynasty (the Qing) injected considerable energy into the commercial and agricultural economies, enjoying particular success in exporting tea, porcelain, and finished silk fabric. In the last half of the eighteenth century under the Manchus, China was an ascendant power with a strong sense of integration under its emperor.

By the nineteenth century the Qing rulers, like the dynasties before them, began to fail. Corruption permeated the routes to official position, and the military was neglected. Conditions deteriorated for the poor. Altogether the regime began to flounder and the former hostility to the Manchu foreigners escalated.

What brought all these trends together was a series of very public and terrifying setbacks. First came the Opium War (1839–1842). In trading with the Chinese, the British had found that flooding China with opium was a way to keep the trade in balance. As the English imported much more from China than the reverse, they used drugs to provide equity. When the Qing objected, war broke out and Western powers revealed China's military weakness and established protected zones there for Western commerce. Opium sales soared. Far more destructive and problematic was the Taipei rebellion (1850–1864) which, though propelled by a very ruthless group, promised serious improvements as well as uplifting of society along Christian lines. Although subdued eventually, the uprising revealed the inherent weakness of the regime and the loss of authority for Confucian ways. Finally, defeat in war by Japan in 1895 showed that even former tributaries that had previously had to conciliate Chinese emperors could in fact stand up to the Manchu rulers.

Despite continuing efforts at reform, the reigning dynasty simply had lost credibility. Already having in 1906 abandoned Confucian principles for staffing the government, the Qing had little resilience and relatively minor setbacks encouraged rebellion. So incompetent and battered by foreign defeats had Manchu rule become that the regime disintegrated by 1912 from defections throughout society, much as the Romanovs would do only five years later. In fact, the first purpose of China's Nationalist Party was to unseat the Manchus and replace them with those of Han descent. After substantial turmoil, more a constellation of mutinies and a coup than a war, the republic was established. Only in 1927 did the Nationalists—whose founding leader, Sun Yatsen, admired Lenin's ideas concerning the evils of imperialism and the need for rule by a vanguard party but rejected Marxist notions of class struggle in favor of a vision of harmony among all members of Chinese society—overcome regional authorities, the "warlords," who held real power at that time. Until Sun Yatsen's death in 1925, the Nationalists collaborated with the Communists and received help from Soviet advisers. In the effort to consolidate authority in 1927, though, Sun's successor, Chiang Kai-shek, attacked the Communists, eliminated their urban leadership and drove the rest to isolated strongholds far north and west of China's great coastal cities. During the Second World War, to resist the Japanese invaders, the two parties, now led by Chiang and Mao Zedong, respectively, forged an uneasy truce and collaboration, but after 1945 they resumed their civil war, which culminated with the Communist triumph in 1949. A second revolution then occurred in the social and political realms. Thus, to comprehend revolutionary ideas as they developed in China, requires an examination first of the Nationalists and then of their opponents.

Political allegiances still play a large role in how commentators interpret Mao and Chiang. This section attempts to explain their ideas and plans as dispassionately as possible without systematically considering the human costs of such changes.

The beliefs of the nationalists remain difficult in part to chart, because Sun Yatsen, a key figure in the 1911 Revolution as well as later events, in his attempts to create a nation, had to seek supporters in many places. To understand the state of his mature thinking, we may well begin with the background to his plan laid out in 1924 for a new political and social regime.

Nineteenth-century China, like Europe, held many people contemplating reform or revolution. With the Manchu government widely unpopular, reformists of many opinions competed. Emerging as most important in this political ferment was Sun who, born in 1866, had spent four years as a teenager at school in Hawaii where he lived with his brother. By his early twenties, Sun was interested in politics and focused on unseating the monarchy. At considerable risk, he found support to finance a revolution whose goal was to create a republic in a united China. The time and effort he expended suggest that he believed these political goals had become absolutely central for the modern Chinese nation. Yet when the Manchus abdicated, no true republic emerged, and within months of taking on the role of China's first president, Sun was forced to cede power to military strongman Yuan Shikai, a former Qing general turned supporter of the revolution. Indeed, neither republic nor unified state would exist until after Sun's death in 1925. Yet in the effort to change the government, Sun emerged as the most prominent republican and launched in 1911 the Nationalist Party (Kuomintang, or KMT for short), which in the decade after his death created a national government.

In Sun's thought and activism, the main focus was political but always included social goals. His thought was eventually encapsulated into "The Three Principles of the People." The first principle was nationalism, which to the Chinese indicated ethnic nationalism. Free from imperial domination, the Chinese ethnic groups would form a single nationality. Although modern-day scholars believe such ethnic identification already existed in China, Sun wanted to identify and solidify such allegiances and used the first flag of the republic to symbolize such by including each of five main participating ethnic groups with a particular color. The second principle was "democracy," while the third was the welfare of the people, which Sun usually called socialism. Sun's oft-stated Principles were open to widely varying interpretations. In 1924, just before his death, he spelled out their meaning to him in a series of sixteen speeches totaling more than 500 printed pages (in translation). This statement of principles marked a high point in his definition of them. Much influenced by the Bolshevik revolution, Sun at this time received tutoring directly from a representative of the Comintern as he laid out his political goals.

Consistent with other emanations of his opinions, Sun sketched a beleaguered race of 400 million people, who dated back to an ancient civilization, but were in danger of extinction because of stagnant population growth. Compared to Western nations whose populations were exploding and economies booming, China was floundering. And he predicted that the next war would not be based on racial distinctions but would have a social cast, with the capitalist countries attacking Russia.

Sun continued to be concerned about Chinese weaknesses, including serious military defeats by Japan and losing border skirmishes with Russia. Furthermore, surrounding countries such as Nepal, Bhutan, and Ceylon, although too small to attack China, were competing effectively and hampering the Chinese economy. If the Chinese could not respond quickly, they would face the plight of Native Americans. As Sun sought a solution, he declared that China was facing chaos because of too much liberty, and he outlined his response: the republic would hold elections, including the right of recall and referendum. Administrators would consist of five units—judiciary, legislature, executive, examinational, and censorial. Sun's explicit admiration for Soviet Russia and Bismarck's Germany indicated his emphasis on order more than democracy, though this did not stop the wildly eclectic Sun from claiming at times that his Principles corresponded to 1789s Liberté, Égalité, and Fraternité and Lincoln's Government of the people, by the people, for the people.

In some lectures, he discussed the third principle—socialism. In general, Sun most often described his plans that more resembled the welfare state's safety net than either socialism or communism, as commonly defined. At a school to organize farmers for the party, Sun indicated his social thinking in 1924. Although his Comintern handler repeatedly urged him to develop a confiscatory and redistributive policy taking from the rich to give to the poor, Sun remained hesitant. He agreed that landlords squeezed the peasants dry, but he believed that a radical policy would have to wait until enabled by social conditions. Farmers should join the national struggle but not class struggle. Rural problems required peaceful cooperation among the government, farmers, and landowners. Sun urged caution on the student organizers and prescribed persuasion and deliberation to solve issues so that "the farmer will benefit and the landlord not suffer loss ...." Nonetheless, his final objective remained that the "tiller shall have his land, receive the results of his labor, and not have it seized by another."[5] Sun's temporizing and vacillation on the social issue show that he was by no means a committed Marxist or would-be Bolshevik.

The death of Sun Yatsen (March 12, 1924) opened the way for others to consolidate national power. Inheriting the real power in the KMT, the ruthless military leader Chiang Kaishek continued the drive to unite the nation. Enormously successful, Chiang cemented the KMT's power in southern China, then, after defeating some Northern Warlords, arrived in Beijing in 1928. With the country largely united under his party, he moved the capital to Nanjing where the Ming dynasty, the last ethnic Chinese one, had reigned, symbolically fulfilling Sun's ideal. Chiang's rule largely ended warlordism. Although he had collaborated with some of these strongmen in his military drive north, eventually he turned on them and consolidated his authority and that of the KMT over most of the country.

In the years before the Japanese attack in 1937 on the Chinese heartland (Japan had already seized Manchuria in 1931), Chiang proved himself a modernizer but no socialist. Under his rule, the great powers recognized the Chinese currency, and some of the government weaknesses in foreign affairs were eliminated. The economy modernized; educational opportunities increased. Nonetheless, Chiang continued to do little to improve the plight of the peasants. His connections to the landlords inhibited reform. Business preyed on the poor, as traders and moneylenders provided allegiance to the government in return for no reform. Economic injustice as well as a continued political monopoly and chronic budget deficits left the country internally unstable and internationally insecure.

However, the Communists remained a problem for the KMT. Many commentators and historians have endeavored to explain the coalition and conflicts between these two rivals. The Comintern was pressuring Sun, but the Communists as well, to embrace united front activities. With Sun's prestige and ambiguous but potentially left leaning socialism, the coalition was imaginable. Still, the Chinese communists held that the party should represent the workers, at least in theory, and the KMT advocated a multiclass future. KMT inaction on peasant issues also contributed to division. Such differences made for an uneasy coalition which, when opportunity and potent disagreements arose, Chiang dissolved in 1927, abruptly attacking his erstwhile allies. Scholars have debated the cause of this breakup, which led to the massacre of thousands of Communists and the virtual elimination of the party in the heavily populated areas of China. Perhaps, the most reasonable explanation is that both sides were looking to their own advantage and little trust existed, once the unifying figure of Sun was dead. In any case, after the defeat, Mao Zedong, a rising political leader, escaped with 1,000 followers to the mountains of Jiangxi, some 300 miles from the battle. The party limped along, almost disappearing by 1930, but a remnant continued to survive in the mountains. In 1934, Chiang incited an

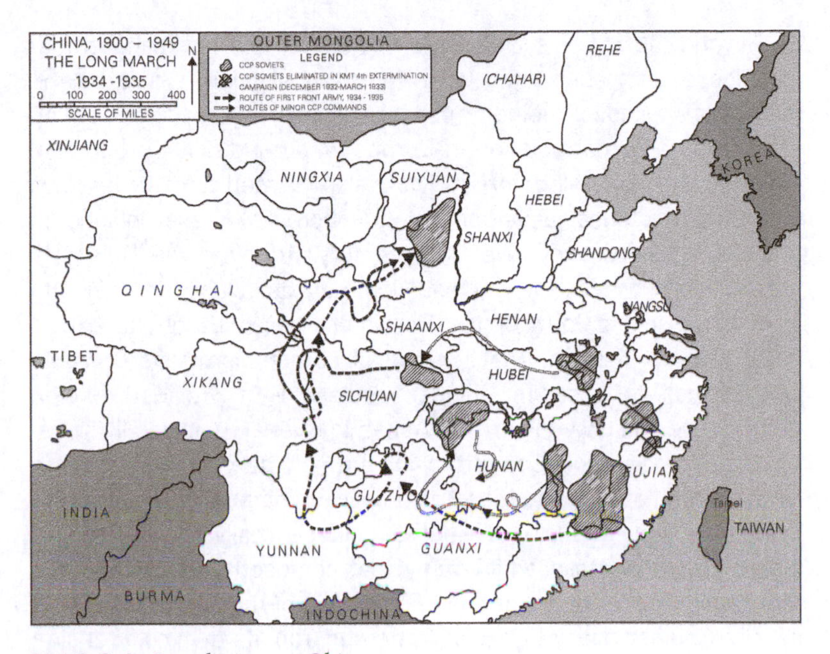

MAP 3.1 *Revolutionary China.*

Driven from eastern cities, the Communists regrouped far from the dense concentrations of population.

effort to destroy the Communist remnant. But Mao, by that point an increasingly important military leader, the army, and the future of Chinese Communism survived, as he helped lead a retreat that moved operations on a Long March (really marches) of some 6,000 miles to isolated Shaanxi province, and no doubt, made a social revolution still possible, however remote (see Map 3.1).

The Communist Party

With Chiang Kaishek in control, it would fall to the Communists to make a social revolution, if one were to occur. And, in fact, in 1934 the urban Communist Party was dispersed and those surviving were far from the populace and seats of power. A treacherous road awaited the Chinese Communists before they succeeded in 1949 to implement a socialist regime focused on the peasantry.

Beyond the sheer scale of the change lay the unlikelihood that a Chinese party associated with European Marxism would be the source of a takeover fueled by peasant soldiers and support. Coming from an intellectual tradition in Europe where industrial production seemed to sweep all before it, Marx also claimed to discover laws of human historical development that bore little resemblance to the China of the early twentieth century. Admiring the Bolshevik Revolution from afar, the Chinese Communists still had to deal with it at home in the form of the Comintern which sought to export the Bolshevik version. That version of communism was unstable and difficult to apply in Chinese society as it provided foreign perspectives on how to seize power amid Russian political divisions. As noted above, the Comintern increasingly served the Kremlin's shifting international priorities. To complicate matters still more in the 1920s and early 1930s, it presented an ideologically framed political battle between Stalin and Trotsky that confused and complicated the ideological development and positioning of the Chinese classes. Finally, Chinese nationalist goals emerged from its own chief desire: the desire to repulse Western and Japanese imperialism. Yet this unlikely union with the Marxist tradition in China yielded potent results over the long haul.

Understanding how the Chinese adopted and changed the Russian version of Marxism begins with Chen Duxiu and Li Dazhao—generally considered the founders of the party—and its later preeminent leader, Mao Zedong. Although the founders held rather different conceptions of socialist policy, they shared the problems of fitting together different understandings of communism in the evolving Chinese party.

Born in 1888 to a rural middle-class family, Li, an early idealist and patriot, explored the panoply of groups promising renewal and change. Although some of the intelligentsia disliked capitalism, they tended to view socialism as a distant but not especially relevant goal. Even after the Russian Revolution made Marx and Lenin's thought more prominent, the Chinese found such concepts difficult to absorb because of their meager experience with Marxian terms and concepts. The student uprising of May 4, 1919, in Beijing, a protest against the government's weak response to the Versailles settlement that ceded territory to Japan, radicalized many. Li had already embraced the Russian Revolution, which attracted him because its internationalism and sudden victory provided new hope that China might quickly advance. Here Lenin's belief in uneven development opened the door to the view that China, in struggling against imperialism, had been welded into a "proletarian" nation and could thus be transformed through the action of the Communists. By claiming that this struggle with the West was racially based, Li could further energize and nationalize the struggle to include all Chinese classes.

While embracing Marxism–Leninism for its potential to transform China, Li did not hesitate to innovate. Like the Russian Bolsheviks, the Chinese had to modify Marx's concepts in order to make this revolutionary paradigm relevant to the circumstances of a largely agrarian nation. Even while Li embraced Russian Marxism because of the dramatic changes available through the power of the Party, he also had to explain how China, an economically backward nation, could be ready for socialism. Committed to a belief that a socialist society could be built on the basis of the peasantry, Li found support in those like Plekhanov, who earlier in a populist vein had embraced the role of the peasants. In Lenin's theory of uneven development, the peasantry always remained subordinate to the proletariat. Trotsky had implied some role for the peasantry in his notion of permanent revolution, and he reiterated that point after Lenin's power waned with fading health. Nonetheless, even for Trotsky, the peasants were subordinate. His reaffirmation of permanent revolution nevertheless circulated in China and received approbation from many. The small size of the Chinese industrial laboring force made it impossible for the Communists to rely on the urban workers, and Li fully engaged rural laborers. Li averred that spontaneously the peasantry would reach "class" consciousness, though perhaps he meant "national" consciousness with the Party assigned to guide them. Li's earlier faith in the people and their ability to achieve political understanding drove him toward the Leninist view that the workers would accept the dominance of the party, but Li was perhaps more generally optimistic than the Russian (and more "Marxian") in regard to the laboring classes' intelligence especially that of peasants whom Lenin had cast in the role of "followers," unlike the proletariat which could be linked to the party and even able in the party to rise to its leadership.

Nominally Li's superior, Chen Duxiu, had created the Chinese Communist Party in 1921 and was its first designated leader. Just as in the Russian party, different points of view coexisted at least at first, without the threat of violent purges. Although from a family of officials, Chen (1879–1942) shared the widespread disappointment with China's deteriorated conditions as the Qing dynasty lurched to its end. Underlying all his actions was a desire to replace an archaic system with a vital, energetic Chinese nation. Trained as an intellectual, Chen first worked as a scholar to effect his goal. Through this medium, he made his political contribution by attacking Confucian ideas and intellectual foundations. He designed his revision of punctuation to upstage past conventions and intended a political impact. This paralleled the republicans in the 1912 revolution who used culture to make a revolutionary statement about rejecting the past and embracing Westernism by cutting off the Manchu queue (ponytail) and adopting Western styles.

In 1921, Chen and a small group of Marxist intellectuals founded the Communist Party. While his prestige as a scholar and his intellectual prowess as a mandarin brought luster to his new party, he disparaged those people for whom he was creating a party:

> ... a partly scattered, partly stupid people possessed of narrow-minded individualism with no public spirit who are often thieves and traitors and for a long time have been unable to be patriotic, so there is no point in talking of anything further ....[6]

Evidently he deeply doubted the people's ability at self-government: "Obviously the more people in a nation who will take responsibility the better, but among this kind of irresponsible people with no ability, purpose or knowledge, to give them responsibility is to commit national suicide. In China at this time not only is government by the whole people worthless to talk of but it is a dream."[7] Even Lenin, whose *What Is to Be Done?* severely questioned the acumen of workers, would have refrained from voicing such an extraordinary lack of confidence, and his emphasis was to remedy any failure of the people through Marxism–Leninism. Unlike Lenin, Chen would leave leadership open within the Chinese Communist Party and even included non-Marxian socialists or anarchists who joined the party to carry out economic reform and enhance productivity.

What was the party in power supposed to do? Although Chen saw the ultimate goal in completely orthodox terms as the rule of the proletariat and the end of capitalism, he held other views that complemented and even contradicted these. According to historian Lee Feigon, Chen knew little of Marxist–Leninism and was not rigorous in his interpretation. And he had very unusual ideas about the Marxist stages of development. Although he agreed to cooperate with the bourgeois KMT because he believed that this class would develop productivity, he argued that the Communist Party must immediately create through violent revolution the economic conditions for the destruction of capitalism and the creation of maximal productivity. The bourgeoisie would not fulfill its historic role; and counter to Lenin, Chen assumed that the laboring class would do this on its own without outside aid. Consequently, despite his low opinion of cultivators, he, more than others before Mao, advocated an expanded role for the peasants in the revolution. Chen wanted more of a broad-based party and was more assertive about the role of the peasants than was Li; but in the end they agreed that agrarians could provide the backbone of revolution. This emphasis on the peasants foreshadowed the ideas of other communist revolutionaries in nonindustrial and colonized societies.

Life did not end pleasantly for Chen or for Li. Trapped in Beijing in 1927 as the KMT forces occupied the city and rooted out the Communists, Li was arrested when troops stormed the Soviet Embassy. Held in seclusion for nearly two weeks, he was executed by strangulation. Although Chen died in his bed in 1942, he had first been ousted as head of the Party and later placed under arrest by the Nationalist (KMT) government for five years. He spent a few years in retirement in poor health before his death. In those last years, he resumed his former more moderate beliefs and even embraced liberal democracy. His renunciation of communism, for which he had sacrificed so much, must have been personally painfully.

Mao Zedong became a communist and like Li and Chen took the Chinese party far from its European Marxist roots. Born into a middling peasant family in 1893, in his early years he was attracted to anti-imperialism and, influenced by Chen Duxiu in particular, joined the Communist Party at its inception. In 1927 his independent role began and flourished. Mao proved to be an extremely successful organizer. Although he had constantly battled with the party, he emerged as a leading figure in military struggles with the KMT. By 1934, after more than a decade of fighting and difficulty, Mao's forces, as noted above, escaped to an isolated part of north-central China. From these exploits, Mao had risen to the preeminent position in the party. Civil war with the KMT would continue but was also punctuated by eight years of uneasy cooperation to expel the Japanese from 1937 until the surrender in 1945. Following the defeat of the invaders, Mao and his forces managed to decisively defeat the KMT in the Civil War (1945–1949). He remained head of the Chinese Communist Party until his death on September 9, 1976.

Mao's thought took many twists and turns. Only the broad outlines of his thinking as it developed up to the Great Leap Forward (1958–1959) and the Cultural Revolution (1966–1976) may be considered here, along with a coda on these two events.

Mao faced some of the same intellectual problems as had Lenin, Trotsky, and his Chinese predecessors: how could a socially and economically backward country be ready for a proletarian revolution? First, and most important for the long run, Mao consistently and even passionately believed that the objective conditions for each nation mattered. Resentful of the interference of the Comintern, he argued for the "sinification" of the revolution, or, in other words, adapting the revolution to Chinese circumstances. In the case of China, he believed conditions to be ripe. In his view, the party would instill revolutionary consciousness in the proletariat, which in turn would teach it to the peasants, who then would become proletarians. What made this era pregnant with possibility was the success of the Russian Revolution. Although a foreign event, its implications were tremendous for China's rebellious peasantry, hardened by war with the KMT and then the Japanese. The success of the Bolshevik consolidation of power in the 1920s allowed Chinese to believe in the reality of a just dictatorship. For them it would include participation from *all* classes, creating a unified dictatorship. Once power was achieved, its hallmarks would include centralization under the party coupled to the "mass line" (the popular instinct)—the return of political elites to the values of the masses. This would guarantee that the leaders would be listening to the masses and acting with the proper values. This certainly was a more inclusive approach than Lenin, though Stalin had come, at least in theory, to some of the same positions. Instead of democracy, the party would emphasize communication, participation, and peasant–party interaction, and Mao's economic goal always emphasized industrialization.

Although Mao had emphasized the positive, though not leading, role of the peasant in the road toward socialism, he changed his focus toward this class in the middle 1950s with his "Great Leap Forward." Agriculture, mainly through the reorganization of communes, investments, and untested schemes, even in the area of industry, should become the source of the growth and development of the proletariat to support the necessary economic substructure for socialism. Explanations for Mao's changed policies abound, but no one questions that his initiative had great impact. To those who decried his plans, he noted that the peasants wanted change and like "a clean sheet" had no "blotches so the newest and most beautiful words can be written upon it ...."[8] Dearth, famine, and millions of deaths followed, as well as resistance in the countryside, all of which led to the formal end of the policy in 1962. Not tiring of experimentation and believing in permanent revolution, Mao launched the Cultural Revolution in 1966 as an attack on intellectuals and technical experts whom he thought did not help the proletariat. This obviously assailed members of the party and was inextricably linked to Mao's view of the role of the masses. Mao denounced those who opposed the masses and countenanced attacks from the Red Guards (students, revolutionaries, peasants, workers, soldiers, and low-level functionaries) against their "enemies." The Great Leap Forward and the Cultural Revolution, somewhat similar, had the same result—the deaths of many, perhaps even several millions. Together they also gave further impetus to a populism that expressed Mao's enduring embrace of the masses, particularly the peasants, who considerably outnumbered their peers in the cities.

As Rebecca Karl has insightfully argued, the Cultural Revolution and the Great Leap Forward opened new ground in communist thinking. By turning to the masses to innovate economically and culturally, Mao was in fact turning on Party leadership other than himself. The Party was reduced to just one man who would then reshape and reorganize activities with the input from below.[9] This national experiment was an extremely convulsive experience that likely profoundly shaped the relationship between the Party and the public. Certainly Mao created an interlude in which initiative had relocated more than for any of his predecessors but might have been closest to the secular worker heaven foreseen by Marx, had it not had such disastrous consequences in the real world.

In sum, both Chinese and Russian Communists evolved far beyond Marxism as expressed in the *Communist Manifesto*; but the Chinese thought and policies proved more important in their era. Marx's great polemical pamphlet had justified revolution, but his doctrine assumed specific economic conditions and strictures. The Russian and Chinese revolutions deepened the tendency for Marxists in different national contexts to freelance, choose among, and improvise upon Marx's tenets. Above all, the Leninist concept and practice of a highly centralized Communist Party reconfigured the idea of revolution. Even though the Chinese Cultural Revolution temporarily undermined the party, it did not in any way criticize the concept of the dictatorship of the proletariat. The new revolutionary movements would be led by centralized parties using highly coercive methods of control. As noted, Chinese communists took more latitude in using Marxist thought to empower a mass movement, and Mao very deliberately subordinated the party to the mass-line, overwhelming the formal party with mass involvement. More systematically, the Chinese created an ideology that matched up far better to their agrarian world than the Russian version. By favoring the peasantry and also claiming from the revolution's early beginnings that resistance to imperialism created class consciousness, these ideological notions also could relate to the circumstances in most of Asia and Africa at the end of the Second World War. In addition, the overt Chinese practice of the revolution as national, especially their temporary compact with the KMT to put aside socialism in order to drive out the invader, could make Marxism appear relevant to purely nationalist movements. This book, which seeks to narrate the global idea of revolution, suggests that Lenin's attack on imperialism and more generally the Chinese revolution's revision of Marxist ideology kept these concepts at the forefront of the revolutionary movements of the colonized societies of Asia and Africa.

The Communists admired Robespierre and the Jacobins. Did they really understand them?

Essay 3

Rosa Luxemburg and Vladimir Lenin: *What Is to Be Done?*

Focusing as this book does on the thought and general practice of revolutions inevitably overplays the role of the leadership—and that means men, mainly white. Beyond those peaks of the movement were many, many women who played a visible role or embraced such ideas of change. Gender expectations that were manifest in movements embracing violence almost guaranteed that women could not enter leadership. And certainly history itself, with its own gender biases, has overlooked many interesting stories.

Even by the middle of the nineteenth century, a burgeoning woman's movement had arisen, peopled mainly by women who, while not yet generally challenging the traditional family, sought among other rights, enfranchisement, entry to many professions, more equal educational opportunities, and expanded legal and custody rights.

Moreover, some women entered the general political realm as activists, and many would name Rosa Luxemburg the most important female socialist theorist of the early twentieth century. Mainly a political philosopher and political revolutionary, and acutely aware of sexist discrimination—but not wishing to marginalize her work in the movement—she commented relatively little on women's issues. Nonetheless, analyzing these remarks allows insights into the Marxian view of women. Further, her political beliefs, in which she took a position different than Lenin, prove very enlightening about the tone and temper of Lenin's essential innovation regarding the role of the party.

Born in Poland in 1871, Luxemburg became a citizen of Germany and heavily participated in radical politics. In opposition to support for the war offered by the Social Democrats, she helped found the Spartacus League that later became the Communist Party. In the midst of a revolt in 1919, she was captured and killed by the German government.

Luxemburg's deepest allegiance was to political change, but she associated herself with women's participation in the movement and sought equal rights there and at the voting booth. She believed that it was the proletarian woman's turn to take on the capitalists. Participation in the socialist movement made women's role valuable. Not surprisingly, she expected little from bourgeois women who, in her opinion, were not an independent segment of the populace. She considered them only co-consumers of the surplus value that men extorted from the populace. "They are parasites .... and co-consumers are usually even more rabid and cruel in defending their right to a parasite's life than the direct agents of class rule and exploitation."[10]

Luxemburg deemed bourgeois woman suffrage movements farcical because they lacked material roots and were but a "phantasm of the antagonism between men and women."[11] Perhaps surprisingly to the modern reader, Luxemburg did not appeal to all proletarian women. To understand the situation of the worker well, she averred that one must be part of the exploited and that meant being a laborer employed by capitalists. Women working at home could not grasp the issues. And she suggested that women should "simply insist on paid work in the economy so they can learn to resist. Indeed, as a modern female proletarian, the woman becomes a human being for the first time." Only the struggle prepared women to contribute to "the best of humanity."[12]

Not supporting all but only those women who had been directly involved in paid employment, Luxemburg focused on class struggle where she placed her greatest emphasis. More socialist than feminist, she deserves evaluation in this role. Comparing her views with Lenin's more clearly reveals the commitment that drove the Russian Bolsheviks and allows the reader to understand also how much closer some Marxists remained to elements of Marx's early concepts.

As discussed in Chapter 3, Lenin departed from the *Communist Manifesto* in regard to the role of the Party, the necessity of passing through the social and economic stages of history in a prescribed order, and the requisite preparedness in terms of class maturity. In subsequent views, as Marx contemplated the subjects, he too reconsidered matters. Luxemburg agreed completely with Lenin's more aggressive timetable to move toward socialism, as she averred in 1918 that although Russia was not, according to theory, supposed to be "ripe for the social revolution,"[13] it was. As the workers themselves had placed all power in the hands of the Soviets, the only positive exit was the seizure of power. In fact, the general uprising of the international proletariat (here Luxemburg referred to significant labor restiveness and turbulence after the First World War) justified a revolution and was "the clearest proof" of the "foresightedness" of the Bolsheviks.[14] Yet this support for action did not deter Luxemburg when it came to criticizing the implementation of various social policies and especially to the organizational centralization launched in Bolshevik Russia. On this last topic, her comments were especially harsh.

Comparing Luxemburg's approach to Lenin's view of centralization requires scrutinizing his understanding of the place of the party and its role in revolution. In 1902, well before even the revolution of 1905, Lenin had articulated his new vision of an elite, secretive party that should lead the revolution. His book, *What Is to Be Done?*, had divided the Russian socialists, but it also informed the Bolsheviks for the next several decades.

In *What Is to Be Done?*, Lenin laid out his vision that Russia faced an incomparably difficult task because of an undersized, undereducated proletariat and the existence of a powerful autocracy. Russian socialists needed vigor and allegiance to their theory. He noted that while progress in science required freedom to discuss antithetical views, complete freedom of criticism had no place in this situation.

The Russian workers, continued Lenin, were simply not able to understand the opportunities. They could grasp the particular injustice but could not understand the overall system from which it issued. Necessary to this process was a party, full of intellectuals who connecting to the proletariat through particularly able workers could constantly transform a complaint about a problem into a broader critique. This would be the way that a spontaneous reaction could turn into a political critique. Further the revolutionaries needed to confront the able Tsarist police by this spark.

Lenin argued that to be effective, the groups of workers needed a leader, a "tribunal," who could take every incident, no matter how small and "produce a simple picture of police violence and capitalist exploitation."[15] As a liaison to the laborers, the Party must train actual workers who, though not necessarily up to the intellectual level of the party, could through their activity lead agitation and action. Some areas were so sophisticated that they required intellectuals who were dedicated professional revolutionaries. Lenin was clearly aware of the apparent hierarchy he was imposing and the values underlying it when he noted that workers should not be offended by his remarks, since he at first had been lacking in revolutionary sophistication. Here he permitted workers a path into the party but, based on the many pages focusing on their exclusion, it seemed to be a very narrow one. Clearly, however, the Bolsheviks did become more open to amalgamating workers into the party as evidenced by the change in personnel and leadership over time. Yet, as clearly argued by Lars Lih in his extremely positive view of Lenin, the openness toward workers did not include ending the commitment to a conspiratorial nonpublic party.

Rosa Luxemburg opposed this vision of a conspiratorial party continuing indefinitely after the seizure of power. While noting that Russia had special circumstances that justified such policies—agricultural land division, a different approach toward the nationalities, for example—she rejected justifications for such an elite party and she focused on critiquing Lenin's conception of the party. Luxemburg believed that once power had been seized, democracy must begin in building socialism. She agreed that a dictatorship would exist, but it "consists in the manner of applying *democracy*, not in its *elimination*."[16] Luxemburg conceded that such a dictatorship would tear down the regime of the bourgeoisie, but she passionately asserted the need for democracy and freedom. Indeed, "the danger begins only when they [Bolsheviks] make a virtue of necessity and want to freeze into a complete theoretical system all the tactics forced upon them by these fatal circumstances, and want to recommend them to the international proletariat as a model of socialist tactics."[17]

Along with this critique and plan for the future, Luxemburg lyrically defended the value of freedom and democracy in a way that one cannot imagine Lenin doing. Democracy was necessary because in that crucible the masses exerted their influence. She deemed the approach of Lenin and Trotsky to be wrong because "it stops up the very living source from which alone can come the correction of all the innate shortcomings of social institutions. That source is the active, untrammeled, energetic political life of the broadest masses of the people."[18] In further distinction from the Bolsheviks, she extolled the value of freedom of inquiry. Trotsky argued that the laboring masses were already sufficiently knowledgeable, so no new knowledge was necessary. Given Lenin's early and continuous support for party supremacy and discipline, Trotsky's vision seems at best expedient, but Luxemburg did not directly mention this but instead noted that if his view was correct, why shut off the masses the moment the Bolsheviks seize power? And she interposed:

> Freedom only for the supporters of the government, only for the members of one party—however numerous they may be—is no freedom at all. Freedom is always and exclusively freedom for the one who thinks differently. Not because of any fanatical concept of "justice" but because all that is instructive, wholesome and purifying in political freedom depends on this essential characteristic, and its effectiveness vanishes when "freedom" becomes a special privilege.[19]

All these insights from Luxemburg throw Bolshevik centralizing into even sharper relief. As the protagonists disagreed about the role of the party, their differences became more surprising and striking. In fact, framed by Luxemburg's highly idealistic conception of a socialism characterized by freedom and democracy, Lenin's notion seems much more arbitrary and repressive. Nonetheless, separated by borders, political realities, her death, and history, it was Lenin's approach that gained traction among radical socialists, called henceforth by most, communists. More moderate factions would be generally labeled socialist and some became over time more and more moderate, reformist rather than at all revolutionary. Luxemburg's alternative direction, aimed at the future after a successful revolution, perished along with her, at least within the confines of most communist parties.

Rosa Luxemburg and Mao Zedong were more favorable than Lenin to the masses. How did Mao and Luxemburg differ?

Further Reading

Baron, Samuel H. *Plekhanov: The Father of Russian Marxism*. Stanford, 1963.

Bonnell, Victoria. *Roots of Rebellion: Worker Politics and Organization in St. Petersburg and Moscow, 1900–1914*. Berkeley, 1984.

Daniels, Robert V. *Trotsky, Stalin, and Socialism*. Boulder, 1991.

Feigon, Lee. *Chen Duxiu: Founder of the Chinese Communist Party*. Princeton, 1983.

Fitzpatrick, Sheila. *The Russian Revolution*, 2nd Ed. New York, 2001.

Karl, Rebecca E. *Mao Zedong and China in the Twentieth-Century World*. Durham, 2010.

Kraus, Richard Curt. *The Cultural Revolution: A Very Short Introduction*. New York, 2012.

Lih, Lars T. *Lenin*. London, 2011.

Meyer, Alfred G. *Leninism*. New York, 1962.

Read, Christopher. *War and Revolution in Russia, 1914–1922: The Collapse of Tsarism and the Establishment of Soviet Power*. New York, 2013.

Ree, Erik van. *The Political Thought of Joseph Stalin: A Study in Twentieth-Century Revolutionary Patriotism*. London, 2002.

Schram, Stuart. *The Thought of Mao Tse-Tung*. Cambridge, 1989.

Schwartz, Benjamin I. *Chinese Communism and the Rise of Mao*. Cambridge, MA, 1951.

Wade, Rex A. *The Russian Revolution, 1917*. Cambridge, 2000.

Walicki, Andrzej. *Marxism and the Leap to the Kingdom of Freedom: The Rise and Fall of the Communist Utopia*. Stanford, 1995.

Wilbur, C. Martin. *Sun Yat-sen: Frustrated Patriot*. New York, 1976.

4

The Global World of Revolution: Colonialism, Decolonization, and Anti-Western Views

Previously formulated ideas—political rights, legal rights, social change, nationalism, communism, and "vanguard" political parties—continued to fuel revolutions after the Second World War, contemporaneous with and later than the Chinese Revolution. Religion entered politics with a potent new message primarily in the Middle East, and Marxist ideas continue to evolve away from an earlier industrial proletarian past. Furthermore, an anti-Western hostility—as well as elements more selectively chosen from other ideologies—became an essential ingredient in these strong religious and Marxist ideologies. By itself, anti-Western sentiment was important, but alone it could not chart a new future—merely reject a previous one. Nonetheless, many of the new ideas of revolution apparently relied on this anti-Western concept, and this chapter begins with a summary of its origins and dimensions.

Although resentment toward the West, defined to include Western Europe and later its North American offshoots, has deep roots, the focus here is on recent social, political, and behavioral practices—or their caricatures—of the industrial and postindustrial era. First, this version of anti-Western feeling is essentially new.

Although Marxist critics had attacked the feudal past, scorned religion, and found the bourgeoisie scheming, such thinkers had also equated progress with the path pursued in the West. And they certainly had found little of merit in the character of other peoples, at times deeming the "Asiatic" peoples backward. Mao, of course, did not accept the latter position, but he did not strictly oppose modernity as understood by the West. He simply believed in better alternatives to the Western path.

The origins of modern anti-Westernism mainly stem from the long-term effects of colonization. European powers, like other societies, had long sought to expand at the expense of their neighbors. After the game-changing voyages of Columbus, the Atlantic-facing countries of England, Spain, Portugal, France, and Holland all sought colonies in the Americas. As we have seen, this effort spectacularly collapsed at the end of eighteenth and beginning of the nineteenth centuries—as independence movements swept the New World.

Absorbed by Napoleonic wars and their resolution, Europeans paused in overseas expansion, but beginning in 1830 France crossed the Mediterranean and subdued Algeria, thereby launching a new wave of colonial expansion outside of Europe. Eventually, all the former colonizing powers, joined by the Germans, Belgians, Italians, and Americans, held colonies, although Spain and Portugal only retained some earlier conquests. The Ottomans and Russians were "landmass" colonizers, or imperialists as they called themselves. By 1900 almost all of Africa and Southeast Asia—a huge area home to hundreds of millions of people—had been colonized. The extraordinary nature of this extension of power is evident when one considers that the Belgian Congo was eighty times the size of Belgium with a far larger population as well (see Map 4.1). In addition, some scholars have included the American West as a colonized territory of "landmass," expanding colonial power, as seen from the point of view of Native Americans. Taking the point of view of aboriginal populations would add other nations to this list of colonizing powers.

To generalize about this heterogeneous experience of European domination would be nearly impossible. Furthermore, this is a highly disputatious area of scholarship. To understand the situation, a reader has to account for chronology, different imperial powers, different colonized areas, different scholarly assumptions, and most important,

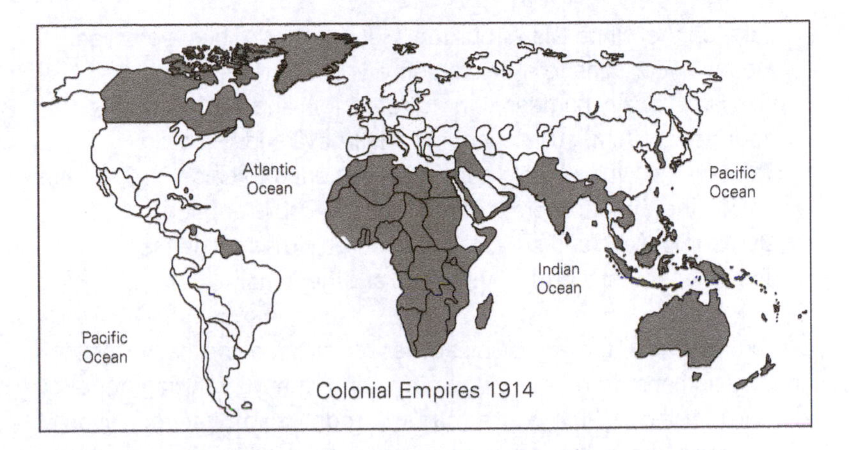

MAP 4.1 *Colonial Empires, 1914.*
European powers and Japan dominated the globe. Although home countries generally enforced their will on the colonized, some exceptions existed, especially Britain's "white" colonies like Canada.

varying sources of documents—whether those of colonized people or of the colonizers. To avoid many of these problems, scholars have tended to focus on a single imperialist power and "its" possessions. This leads to a very chaotic picture.

Nonetheless, it is possible to chart the rise of anti-Western sentiment in general terms. In regard to the acquisitions in Asia and Africa, the European powers were at first confident that bringing Christianity to the heathens would be immensely helpful. Perhaps the apotheosis of this attitude could be expressed in the terms "white man's burden" and "civilizing mission." This latter term, used by the Portuguese and the French, puts forward the notion that association between the colonizer and the colonized, even across different races, was an important goal. Thus, the French, as this empire expanded, sometimes allowed the colonies to vote and send representatives to the national assembly. Rudyard Kipling's "The White Man's Burden" was a famous poem, written in 1899 to encourage the American colonization of the Philippines. It warned of resentment from the occupied, but still advocated that the colonizing nation bear all costs in order to bring economic and cultural enlightenment. One can see his tone in two initial verses:

> Take up the White Man's burden, Send forth the best ye breed
> Go bind your sons to exile, to serve your captives' need;
> To wait in heavy harness, On fluttered folk and wild—
> Your new-caught, sullen peoples, Half-devil and half-child.
> Take up the White Man's burden, In patience to abide,
> To veil the threat of terror And check the show of pride;
> By open speech and simple, An hundred times made plain
> To seek another's profit, And work another's gain.

Not surprisingly, the arrival of armies to subdue the native people met resistance from the beginning, and the patronizing tone of those referring to "the white man's burden" also offended. Even if few among the colonized read this poem, many experienced the European air of superiority that infused this work. Nonetheless, the level of resistance scarcely slowed European expansion. And, indeed, these foreign powers often recruited talented locals into position of responsibility and educated some in Europe, even at elite universities. Such local elites had to balance off personal or social resentments with their own self-interest in economic or professional opportunities and accomplishments.

The momentum of colonialism, powered largely by superior weaponry and constant repression, continued largely unabated until the Second World War, with a high point in the 1920s. The defeated powers in the First World War, the Ottomans, and the Germans were forced to turn over their accessions, which for the former included vast areas of the Middle East—Palestine, Transjordan, the Arabian Peninsula, and more—to the French and the English as "mandates" (see Map 4.2). Even though Europeans had to deal with some restrictions in these new areas, overall colonial authority expanded as the Ottomans probably had ruled more cautiously. These boundaries appeared very settled to faraway observers. A typical map of the period might present England and her possessions in pink, with the French in green, and the map itself the symbol of immense power.

Nonetheless, change was coming from outside colonial authority. Even though Woodrow Wilson did not apply self-determination to the colonies, he made the idea sacrosanct as an international goal. Surely this provided a boost for national liberation, which for India, the most important jewel in the English crown, had already before the war

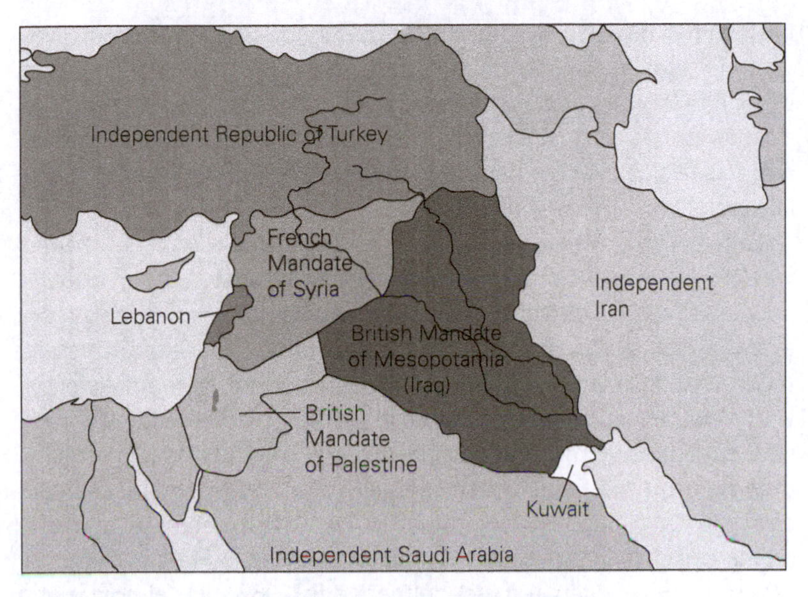

MAP 4.2 *Post–First World War Middle East (1923).*
Even though the vast extent of European colonial holdings in 1914 (Map 4.1) was tested by war, these nations added still more territory through the assignment to France and England of pieces of the former Ottoman Empire.

begun to stir. Indonesia witnessed a similar restiveness. The Second World War itself contributed to new, anticolonial resistance as well. While the West and certainly China deemed cynical the Japanese appeal to create a zone for Asian prosperity, some Burmese may have welcomed this chance offered to create an independent state.

The Second World War accelerated the momentum against colonization; and, by the 1970s, an almost complete decolonization had occurred, excepting those regions adhering to the land mass empires. First, the League of Nations mandates expired, leading to the creation of several independent countries in the Middle East. Moreover, the European powers were shattered, unable to meet the costs of managing the colonies. For example, some English Tories wanted to continue to hold the colonies, but the nation could not afford it because retaining the colonies now required more money than the colonized territories brought to Britain. Costs would exceed profits. Now that funds were required, colonial powers found they could only afford fig leaves that kept the appearance of control, but even that option seemed to be quickly dissipating. Second, the United States, the preponderant power in the West, refused to assist in the direct protection of empires. Last but not least, while the upper classes supported colonialism, the broader public, which became more assertive over the course of the century, did not revel as much in expansion or military glory.

But national freedom did not arrive simply from European weakness; instead it emanated from a long-held desire among colonial peoples to escape outside control. Algeria and Vietnam provide strong evidence for this assertion as France desperately wanted to retain these two colonies. Yet the locals prevailed in an extremely violent war in Vietnam and defeated France in 1954. The United States, which was coming to approve anticommunism more than decolonization, then relieved the French but eventually after significant losses had to settle for a negotiated withdrawal in 1973. Two years later the rebels completely prevailed. A similar fate awaited France in Algeria which eventually secured independence in 1962 after almost eight years of violent struggle. In sum, although separatist movements later emerged in many of the newly independent colonies, the desire for national independence appeared almost everywhere, even when its attainment necessitated prolonged sacrifice.

This turmoil gave rise not only to a rejection of European political control but for many, a decided rejection of the West. In 1902, J.A. Hobson had claimed that the imperialism had been cynically designed, strictly to create captive markets and new products to sell elsewhere. Lenin reinforced this theme in his own book on imperialism. The Comintern even more aggressively depicted colonialism as a rapacious effort to exploit workers. These economic criticisms became common among colonial subjects and even in the West among intellectuals and some government officials. Moreover, a broader critique was emerging about the lands involved. As Europeans reorganized colonial economies, cities grew at the expense of the country. African politicians, in part to curry favor with supporters, decried the despoiling of the land and lamented the loss of the local landscape. In addition, writers such as Frantz Fanon, Aimé Césaire, and Chinua Achebe all attested to the corruption of city life in colonized societies, especially when they contrasted urban centers with the village experience of community. Many intellectuals argued that cooperation was superior to competition in this world, and many anticolonial activists often found socialism more appealing than Western-style capitalism.

Beyond politics and economics, a critique based on race surfaced as an international reaction to European notions of racial dominance. Opposed to beliefs in white superiority, these authors—who often used the term *négritude* (blackness) to promote pride in the history and culture of the black experience—countered white versions of racial thinking. Aimé Césaire became one influential advocate for this kind of race-inflected anticolonialism. Born in the French Caribbean island of Martinique, Césaire gave *négritude* its name in 1935 and thus provided a new analytical framework for many in the colonial world who challenged Western colonial systems. Two other very compelling interpretations and indeed revisions of Césaire's themes came from the Harlem Renaissance in the United States during the early twentieth century and from a new generation of American authors such as Ralph Ellison and Malcolm X.

On a more visceral and daily level, the colonial subjects not only took up specific ideological critiques but also shared an antipathy toward the European presence. With the "owners" of production absent, people had to worry about their jobs in a society where many employers did not regularly live there and did not share in the ups and downs. Furthermore, colonists had to negotiate a political, juridical, and police system that often operated on unfamiliar rules and often in a different language. One might be sent to a war unrelated to local concerns and local wishes. And the privilege of whiteness was not an abstraction but an everyday reality shown by the separate society of private, racially "pure" clubs and "hotels."

Revolutions

Themes of anti-Westernism merged with other post-1945 ideas of revolution, as we can see in the violent political change in the postwar era—though the diverse meanings of this violence are more problematic than one might imagine. Despite the extraordinary number of new nations formed out of colonies (well over fifty), as well as the rash of subsequent upheavals that often displaced the founding leaders of the decolonized nations, most changes did not attain the level of a revolution. Defining revolution as the violent ouster of a sitting government, it would appear that such events happened relatively seldom. Many upheavals achieved revolutionary goals without violence. Even the 1989 upending of Eastern European Communist governments, established and mainly maintained by the Soviet Union, was usually nonviolent. Many British colonies experienced violence, but negotiations played a far more important part in decolonializing most societies. For example, India relied on massive nonviolent demonstrations to pressure British authorities. Other decolonization efforts were characterized by peaceful negotiation or perhaps stoic resignation by exiting colonial officials.

And the causes of change are hardly systematic. Some revolutions, or revolutionary changes that lacked violence, are difficult to relate to decolonization or even the clear echoes of decolonization (Cuba) but formed part of the retreat of Western powers. After breaking free of Spain, though under American sway, Cuba held a number of democratic elections over the decades before the Castro-led revolution. Indirect American pressure, including a brief abortive invasion, had continued in Cuba but not overt colonization. Other factors provided the source of discontent.

In these complex circumstances, many revolutions, as defined in this book, still occurred, though not all were anti-Western. As this book employs a particular definition of revolution to include violence and progressive change, two sets meet and exceed the standard: the Marxist revolutions of Vietnam and Cuba and the politically religious revolution of Iran with its different echoes during the Arab Spring and the Islamic State. Moreover, among the Marxists, it is important to examine the ideas of Martinique-born, Algerian-based Frantz Fanon who, mixing Marxian ideas with anticolonial notions, played a more important role as intellectual than activist. Fanon emphasized anti-Western sentiments, which were not universally accepted among Marxists.

Marxism

After 1945 in the ferment that created many new nations and sought social change, Marxist thought and its direct offspring in Russia and

China, adopted novel usages. Case studies can allow us to chart the dimensions of Marxist thought as it evolved over those decades. One direction of Marxism requires explanation. After 1917, much of the movement in the West, dismayed by the radical elimination of party democracy in Russia, the foreshortening of evolutionary stages, and the violent nature of the Russian regime, formally established nonrevolutionary Marxist parties—known generally under the name of Social Democracy. Eschewing revolutionary change, they lie outside this study. Yet what such parties yielded in the commitment to revolution enabled them to achieve power in many European countries over the last century.

By the second decade of the twenty-first century only four officially designated Communist states—China, Cuba, North Korea, and Vietnam—still existed. The Cuban and Vietnamese examples remained especially important, however, because these two revolutionary nations survived and long received wide coverage in the world press. Their versions of communism illustrated how Marxian ideas were interpreted for a world audience, whether hostile or receptive. Concluding this section is an analysis of Frantz Fanon whose mix of Marxist and anti-Western notions reached beyond Algeria to influence youth movements and would-be revolutionary movements (the "New Left") throughout the Western world.

Together, these examples give some idea of the way that Marxism as a stream overflowed its banks and adopted ideas that Marx himself, and Lenin at times, mainly did not arrive at. This "neo-Marxism" could include nationalism, the elevation of the role of the peasant, and for Fanon race as well. In fact, for the Cubans and Vietnamese, sovereignty was not in doubt, as they accepted their country's boundaries and sought to replace the existing powers with the masses, as they defined this group.

The deep roots of the Vietnamese revolution extend back before the First World War when its young future leader Ho Chi Minh began to consider revolutionary notions, which in his native French-controlled Indochina (composed of modern-day Vietnam, Laos, and Cambodia), seemed to have little resonance. Still, this nascent Communist party staged some uprisings that were easily quashed. The Second World War opened up great opportunities when Germany, after defeating France in 1940, allowed the puppet Vichy government to administer the colonies. Although the Japanese then overran Indochina, they found it easiest to allow the fellow fascist French state to retain a mutually beneficial control. When Japanese authority disintegrated in 1945, Ho and his colleagues immediately overthrew the weakened French. Regrouping, the French returned in force, put the Communists on the defensive, but eventually lost at a cataclysmic battle at Dien Bien Phu in 1954. Peace brought an unwelcome result from the rebels' viewpoint: the carving off of Laos and Cambodia and the partitioning of Vietnam into separate North and South entities with a promised future election and consolidation. But the election never took place, and the war resumed. A huge American military force aided the non-Communist South, but in 1973 the United States, battered on the battlefield and facing great discontent at home, departed; and the South Vietnam government fell in 1975, resulting in the consolidated nation of Vietnam and the end of thirty years of continuous warfare.

From the very beginning, Ho Chi Minh set as a main goal the freeing of his country. Some scholars have interpreted this as *ipso facto* an anti-Marxist goal. Nationalism—defined as a separate governing structure for each ethnic group—surely contradicted the utopian goal of a world of united workers who together obliterated the national structures that as products of bourgeois revolution had kept them apart. Nonetheless, Marx's expectation that revolution would be made by national groups was clearly shown in the way that representatives from national groups arrived at international meetings. But from that base would issue world revolution. The Russians had made their revolution inside their own national borders, and eventually Stalin accepted the necessity of Russia going forward indefinitely under those conditions. Amalgamating "nationalism," rather than national borders, into Marxist ideology expanded Communist practice. The pragmatism of Lenin and his successors justified political independence as trying to benefit one's countrymen. Outside criticism notwithstanding, a similar fusion of communism and nationalism seems to have been a reflexive move by Ho and his compatriots, a move that over decades they repeatedly endorsed.

Ho linked nationalism to Marxist–Leninist conceptions of politics and the economy. For the most part, given that the seizure of power in northern parts of Vietnam after 1945 occurred largely because of French weakness, the Communists did not feel strong enough at first to seek one-party rule. The revolutionaries issued a Declaration of Independence that announced a Western version of political freedom, but behind the scenes the Communists increasingly were creating a one-party state of an entirely different sort. When General Vo Nguyen Giap unembarrassedly asserted that discussion and debate were encouraged, he very clearly intended the Leninist theme that stressed disciplined party control. His interest in combining discipline and democracy in the army reflected the practice of "democratic centralism." Here Giap noted that his soldiers were educated by the Party to know their roles so that they could not be coerced or deceived. Moreover, they were able to explain matters to other soldiers and could discuss everything with officers, including criticisms. While no subject was off limits, strict discipline must be maintained. The term "internal democracy"[1] reflected Giap's more general view: "Armed with Marxist-Leninist theory full of great vigor, our Party and only our Party could work out correct political and military lines appropriate to the practical conditions of our country, to bring our people's armed struggle to success."[2] The correct line for civilians was unquestioned adherence to socialism, as interpreted by the Leninist-style party. In the wake of Lenin, the breadth of openness varied, and political liberties were more constricted beyond the inner circle.

Vietnamese communists did, in fact, reiterate that the goal of the Party was to benefit the workers and peasants under the leadership of the workers, but they were much more hesitant about the introduction of socialism than political discipline which came earlier and is still maintained in Vietnam, at least as a one-party state. In fact, at first the Communists advanced their program as antifeudal. This approach allowed them to resolutely threaten only the wealthiest landowners and attract all the rest of the society, even at times the bourgeoisie, to their side. Essentially, just as the Jacobin leadership acted in the Terror, political loyalty was the test, not class warfare.

Only after northern Vietnamese independence was secured after 1945 did the Party begin to advocate land reform—land seizures and rent reductions—in order to appeal to the rural population. Even this was reformist, at least to some extent, as the communists targeted only publicly reactionary landlords, and lax enforcement prevailed at the local level. Change continued at a slow but significant pace; after the division of Vietnam and the creation of a nonsocialist regime in independent South Vietnam, 800,000 northerners relocated there. An outburst of seizures occurred in the North, and shortly afterward, thousands, after having their property expropriated, were humiliated and some executed. Local officials and possibly senior party officials encouraged these outrages, which included popular denunciations and even murders. Only much later did the government turn toward a broader socialism. In 1957, the national government seriously instituted socialist measures that went beyond land reform to include collectivization of agriculture and collectivization or state ownership of business and industries that included 40 percent of such enterprises. In 1959, a national plan, much like that of Russia, was launched. After North Vietnam finally absorbed South Vietnam and introduced similar economic measures there, an enormous emigration to the United States and elsewhere occurred as well as a major economic collapse. Trying to recover from the ill effects of all these innovations, Vietnam introduced "market socialism" in 1986, but economic uncertainty continued.

Vietnamese policies emphasized agriculture and the peasantry. While the Russians and Chinese focused on industrialization as the goal to create the future, the Vietnamese looked elsewhere. In part, they wished to create a political base in an essentially agricultural nation. Moreover, Ho Chi Minh certainly believed that incentivizing and investing in agriculture would raise the standard of living. In any case, state policy veered far from the original Marxist aim of an industrial society.

This slow introduction of socialism of all types occasioned another kind of debate. Critics of Vietnamese communism believe that Ho Chi Minh and his colleagues delayed a necessary process that would have cost them popularity with entrenched interests. Such observers link this to the early emphasis on nationalism, which was popular. Ho relied on a comfortable ideology to normalize his efforts; once popular, he then introduced socialism piece by piece to keep society off balance until he could complete his agenda. Even those who believe that circumstances dictated the pace of his efforts have no documentary proof to refute the criticism. Yet the longevity of the plot—and the hypocrisy involved—would have required a steadfastness of purpose over decades. It appears that Ho was actually sincere about both nationalism and communism. The first seemed natural to him; the second was difficult, so he did that when he could. That he did not announce this whole program from the beginning may have been strategic rather than duplicitous. And he too would have been disappointed with the current economic situation of the Vietnamese, as he introduced socialism to encourage better living conditions.

Although most Spanish colonies gained independence early in the nineteenth century, Cuba's elite was politically comfortable remaining a colony because the white settlers, a minority compared to the enslaved population, feared life without the protection of the Spanish military. Slaves had few means of political expression. Nonetheless, over time the population grew more restive under colonial domination. A revolt in the 1860s foundered, but in the 1890s a new one succeeded, aided in part by a new burst of imperial interest among North Americans, who wanted to extend their power at the expense of the Spanish and assure American influence on a nearby island. After a brief interim government, the United States granted Cuba formal independence in 1902 but also began a long string of interventions that contributed to the Cuban support for the Castro-led revolution in the late 1950s.

Dissatisfaction with the nature of the newly independent Cuban government began to grow almost immediately, and a communist opposition emerged among intellectuals and workers in the 1930s. Rather than the formal communist party, which was tied to Moscow, an independent insurgency spawned the revolution that would topple the sitting government. Emerging as a potent adversary was Fidel Castro (b. 1926), son of a wealthy planter, who took to the mountains and began a guerrilla movement. Working as a lawyer on behalf of the poor, he had become disenchanted with the government and convinced of the necessity for armed insurrection. Naively, in July 1953, he decided to attack a base of 400 soldiers, located over 500 miles from Havana. With a group of around 125 rebels, he launched the assault which was suppressed in just a few days. Captured, Castro was sentenced to fifteen years in prison but served only nineteen months. Three years later he again resumed revolutionary activities, this time with considerable success, and managed to oust Fulgencio

Batista, the US-supported dictator, in January 1959. Castro has remained in power for more than five decades, rapidly transforming the country to socialism in the countryside and in the cities.

To understand the ideas motivating the revolution proves somewhat difficult, though its opposition to the long history of US interventions links it to the wider patterns of anticolonial revolutionary ideas. Although in social and economic matters Castro governed as a communist, he did not at first declare his affiliation. Two short books by Ernesto "Che" Guevara and Régis Debray on the actions and organization of the guerrillas, however, show that in political terms Castro increasingly acted within the communist tradition as his movement developed in the 1950s.[3] And he, as well as his two compatriots, openly embraced Marxism no later than the 1960s. Scholars have seen Guevara as Castro's alter ego, enormously influential on the leader's actions and thinking, until their rupture for undisclosed reasons in 1965. Debray's book, which parallels but deepens Che's analysis, also chronicles the military and political actions of the Cuban revolution. In the book's introduction, Debray asserted that he had substantial opportunity to examine relevant documents and interview veterans of the conflict including Castro. Together these two works explain the Cuban revolutionaries' political and military approach and reveal a significant transformation in the role of the Party that provided examples for later revolutionaries in Latin America.

Che Guevara (1928–1967) became a mythical figure for the Left because of his devotion to guerrilla war, most notably his involvement in revolutions in Guatemala and Bolivia as well as Cuba. Che was everywhere and anywhere, observing and supporting revolution until he was captured and executed by Bolivian troops. Educated at elite French institutions, Debray (b. 1940) studied philosophy with famed philosopher Louis Althusser and later taught in Cuba. After fighting in Bolivia alongside Che, he became very visible as a public intellectual over the following decades as he addressed a wide range of topics. Most visibly, and to many inexplicably, he advocated secularism in the French school system and expressed strong concerns about the situation of Christian minorities in the Middle East.

Understanding the Cuban intellectual innovation requires a review of the trajectory of Marxist thinking regarding the role of the party. In the *Communist Manifesto*, the revolution sprang from elemental social forces so that eventually the bourgeoisie displaced the aristocracy, only to be replaced in turn by the proletariat. Economic forces would virtually guarantee this result. The Party's role was to educate the working classes who themselves would make the revolution and, if a temporary dictatorship were necessary, would exercise it themselves: thus the name—the dictatorship of the proletariat. As we have seen, Lenin found this gradual process impossible and thus substituted the Party as the indispensable ingredient in a takeover process that provided a small, revolutionary elite linked to working-class membership in the Party. The two groups would lead the wider proletariat to socialism. Mao and Ho agreed about a strong Party leadership, but Mao in particular used the masses to keep the party focused in the right direction.

The Cubans took the trend of the post-Marxists still further by making the armed insurrection, not even the masses or Party members, the vanguard and main creator of the revolution. Basing this theory on the different environment, Debray noted that the Cubans faced an unfriendly environment and an attacking army. Thus, they needed to stay in the countryside and strike as often and as unexpectedly as possible. Che and Debray abandoned Marxist class analysis in favor of contingent conditions to justify the army as the main motor of social revolution.

Che and his associates deduced that in such perilous conditions, revolutionary troops must treat peasants as well as possible; yet it was also important to stay as aloof as possible for self-protection. In short, as Che asserted, and Debray seconded, the liberators found it necessary to build not from the base up, but from the "apex down." This approach they labeled the "foco" strategy, meaning "focalization." Specifically, the argument ran that the revolution would proceed, led by "... in Latin America ... the permanent force first (the *foco*), then the regular forces in the vicinity of the *foco*, and lastly or after victory (Cuba) the militia."[4] Here Che put his faith in loyalists not associated with the general population. Under pressure, the guerrillas needed separation from population sources; yet isolated villages could be of assistance. While the peasants' suspicion of outsiders provided some insulation from others who were truly enemies, this group proved insufficient as a shield. Guerrillas must show their strength and reveal the "bluster" of the oppressor. And Che averred that the revolutionaries must sacrifice their own comfort in order to provide an opportunity to "storm" the village in order to propagandize and recruit the populace.

But what should the guerrillas do as they succeeded? Che asserted, and Debray agreed, that a perfect set of circumstances was not necessary. Instead a class struggle would serve as motivation. Because politicians often failed to deliver, a guerrilla force would triumph because it provided the only political leadership showing the way forward. Seeking no new party, the insurrectionists only hoped to destroy party divisions and unify the people around the war and its political objectives. The main focus became the guerrillas: "Eventually, the future People's Army will beget the party of which it is be, theoretically, the instrument: essentially the party is the army."[5] From the struggle came class conflict, not the reverse.

And to the question of how can one be sure that the army will have chosen the right decisions, Debray apparently offered two responses: living in the countryside with all its rigors was the true proletarian experience, so villagers were already appropriately purified. Relating to them guaranteed the army was on the right track. Furthermore, in regard to concern that the peasants would have to be won over to political action, the troops would respond by organizing and creating, in harmony with the physical rigors of the place, appropriate material assistance. Moreover, in this view, the success of the force proved that it was on the right road.

Debray declared: "The people's army will be the nucleus of the party, not vice-versa. The guerrilla force is the political vanguard in a nutshell and from its development a real party can arise."[6] Marx would scarcely have known his own descendants; Lenin might be inclined to support these ideas but would also note the massive transformation from his own understanding of revolutionary change. The armed force now played the role of the centralized party. Without being specific, the peasants' moral purity would provide the model for the new communist society. In short, the Cuban experience deepened the commitment to a top-down leadership and an agrarian focus.

In a book exploring the ideologies of successful revolutions, Fanon fits somewhat uncomfortably. Born in the West Indies and educated in France, he spent much of his adult life in Algeria. Although he witnessed and participated in the Algerian Revolution, his own role was somewhat limited and his ideological point of view only one of many. Furthermore, one may question why he is listed among the Marxist revolutionaries, when scholars often perceived Fanon as opposed, or perhaps indifferent, to Marxian thinking. His compelling, influential book, *The Wretched of the Earth*,[7] nevertheless suggests that he perhaps was more Marxist than often understood. Proof for his compatibility with Marx lies partly in Fanon's participation as a member of the Communist Party in the Algerian revolution. Furthermore, he deserves a place among the key advocates of revolutionary ideologies because he was so highly regarded, if never exactly followed, in such disparate places as sub-Saharan Africa and the "New Left" in North America and Europe. He expressed some of the anti-Western feeling that decolonization produced and promoted it as a revolutionary ideology.

In Martinique, then a French colony and now a French department, Fanon was highly literate in French language and culture. He first left the island as a member of the Free French forces fighting against the Axis powers in the Second World War and was wounded at the front in 1944. After a brief return to Martinique, he went to France and earned a doctoral degree in psychiatry at Lyons. By 1953 he was working at a psychiatric clinic in Algeria where he witnessed the vicious struggle with France. He died of leukemia in 1961, just before Algerians achieved independence.

Although Fanon wrote several books and lectured widely, the book most directly related to the revolution was his *The Wretched of the Earth*, first published in 1961. As foreground, his *Black Skin, White Masks*, first published in 1952,[8] argued that no matter the circumstances, he found that his blackness always affected perceptions of him. Rather than be defeated by that realization, he resolved to be motivated by it and to reshape this identity, prescribed by whites as the other and lesser, into strength, resilience, and an effort to free himself from the expectations of racists. In fact, he broke free from that racism by basing his revolution not against whites but against colonizers.

Unlike Marx, Fanon focused not on the liberation of the proletariat but on the liberation of the colonized. Still, a striking similarity existed.

Marx had viewed the bourgeoisie and proletariat locked in class warfare that would lead to socialism, but Fanon saw the combatants as the settlers and the natives. Fanon did not conceptualize this as a matter of hatred or racism, although either might have been a base cause of the fundamental divide. He believed that the colonized should react to their objective conditions and should rebel because the lives of colonized people created debilitating psychological conflicts. He wrote:

> The colonized world is a world cut in two. The dividing line, the frontiers are shown by barracks and police stations.
>
> The zone where the natives live is not complementary to the zone inhabited by the settlers. The two zones are opposed, but not in the service of a higher unity.
>
> No conciliation is possible, for of the two terms, one is superfluous. The settlers' town is a strongly built town, all made of stone and steel. It is a brightly lit town; the streets are covered with asphalt, and the garbage cans swallow all the leavings, unseen, unknown and hardly thought about. The settler's feet are never visible, except perhaps in the sea, but there you're never close enough to see them.[9]
>
> The settler's town is a well-fed town, an easygoing town; its belly is always full of good things. The settlers' town is a town of white people, of foreigners.
>
> The town belonging to the colonized people, or at least the native town, the Negro village, the medina, the reservation, is a place of ill fame, peopled by men of evil repute. They are born there, it matters little where or how; they die there, it matters not where, nor how. It is a world without spaciousness; men live there on top of each other. The native town is a hungry town, starved of bread, of meat, of shoes, of coal, of light. The native town is a crouching village, a town on its knees, a town wallowing in the mire.[10]

Settlers to justify this division imagined the native town as "quintessential of evil." After this devastating comparison, Fanon reiterated many other dualities in the "manichean" world of colonialism, as he describes it. To him, the chains of capitalism and the balm of Christianity were elements that cemented the colonized in their alternative space.

Fanon believed that only violence could end this impossible state of affairs. But, as noted, this belief paralleled not only the inevitability of violence as in Marx but the impersonality of social processes often present in Marxist analysis. Both sides bent to the necessity of the conflict. Fanon offered as an exemplar Aimé Césaire's account of a riot that ended at the home of a "good" master in which he and the rebel accept the killing of the master as inevitable, not immoral. And the violence when it came in Algeria and elsewhere would be horrific, a response to the terrible violence that the colonizer inflicted on the subjects. Fanon declared, "The starving peasant, outside the class system, is the first among the exploited to discover that only violence pays."[11]

The Wretched of the Earth argued that after this explosion, solidarity within each group would occur rather spontaneously. And the ardor that appeared would guarantee victory and abolish capitalism. Perhaps slightly less utopian than Marx, Fanon imagined that the only just society that could emerge was "socialist," as the only system that insisted that "man is the most precious of all possessions."[12] Otherwise it would be a society where the few who own resources would "regard the nation as a whole with scorn and contempt."[13] How was this transformation to be carried out? The capitalist countries to protect their own commercial interests would pay to create stable, if no longer colonized, societies. Although this end differed from that of Marx, it paralleled the widely held Marxist notion that the more industrialized countries would play a role, this time to save themselves, not to join their brothers in arms as in Marxist theory. Moreover, it was surely the dialectical struggle that produced this result.

Much of Fanon's remaining analysis expressed themes that also appeared in Mao, Ho, and Guevara, the Marxist critics of his own century. Fanon argued that to make and sustain the revolution, one must start with guerrilla action among the isolated peasantry. His argument turned Marx completely on his head, as Fanon noted that the urban workers were those who had benefited, or at least compromised, with the colonizer. He asserted: "the working class has everything to lose; in reality it represents that fraction of the colonized nation which is necessary and irreplaceable if the colonial machine is to run smoothly: it includes train conductors, taxi drivers, [surprisingly] miners, doctors, interpreters, nurses and so on." These workers were in a "comparatively privileged position."[14]

In the cities, the revolution could depend on the *lumpenproletariat*. This group, who lived in shanties away from tribe and clan, would be one of the most radical forces of the revolution. Further, Fanon noted:

> The constitution of a *lumpenproletariat* is a phenomenon which obeys its own logic, and neither the brimming activities of the missionaries nor the decrees of the central government can check its growth. This *lumpenproletariat* is like a horde of rats; you may kick them and throw stones at them, but despite your efforts they'll go on gnawing at the roots of the tree.[15]

Not only Marx, but Marxists were overturned in Fanon's counterclass analysis because the *lumpenproletariat* had traditionally been understood as the traitor to its class. Viewed as depraved, it could be easily corrupted and used against its class brethren. This Marxist hostility to the poorest of the poor had deep roots as the most radical of the French revolutionaries had argued that the aristocrats would deploy "brigands," the destitute and criminal, against the "good" and "virtuous" people. Moreover, the use of the term lumpenproletariat, so intrinsic to Marxist analysis, shows clearly that Fanon knew he was antagonizing the lions of the socialist movement. To Fanon, this approach to the nonproletarian, disenfranchised lower classes made sense because it restated his notion that when the revolution came, it was not a question of what one was personally but what one would become.

Fanon's apostasy did not stop with his "use" of the peasants and *lumpenproletariat*; it continued in his description of a revolution that never referred to a political party. Limited, or dynamic as the followers of Lenin would have it, the Party does not appear. Here, there was neither vanguard nor leadership. Obviously some leadership must have existed, but spontaneity ruled this treatise. Furthermore, when Fanon in describing a successful revolution, mentioned the Party, he pointed out defects and the necessity of guarding against them.

Fanon believed that the new Party should spring from the natives, but he was extremely skeptical that this would occur. Inevitably, in the circumstances of a unitary revolution that would have occurred, he imagined a one-party state system with a leader who at first would be "gentle." But the "dictatorship of that bourgeois individual" would be cynical, unscrupulous, and eventually would evolve into a cult of personality as well—in the thrall of the former colonial power. Fanon described his vision of the new revolutionary government:

> That famous dictatorship, whose supporters believe that it is called for by the historical process and consider it an indispensable prelude to the dawn of independence, in fact symbolizes the decision of the bourgeoisie caste to govern the underdeveloped country first with the help of the people, but soon against them .... The incoherent mass of the people is seen as a blind force that must be continually held in check either by mystification or by the fear inspired by the police force.... The militant is turned into an informer. He is entrusted with punitive expeditions against the villages. The embryo opposition parties are liquidated by beatings and stonings. The opposition candidates see their houses set on fire. The police increase their provocations. In these conditions, you may be sure, the party is unchallenged and 99.99 percent of the votes are cast for the government candidate.[16]

Such a description appears a thinly veiled attack on the behavior of communist parties in power whose leader hailed from a bourgeois background and ended up part of a cult of personality in a nation with little democracy. This attack obviously also implicated Marx and his followers. Fanon's new idea of the revolution broke from Lenin's "democratic centralism" and idealized the disparate lower classes of colonized people making up the lumpenproletariat.

Fanon ended on a note of instruction. In relying on intellectuals whose job it was to lift the "masses," one would err because "Making a political speech is unsatisfactory and useless." Instead he advocated trying "relentlessly and passionately, to teach them that everything depends on them."[17] No single great leader would be enough; making the revolution would require the masses. In short, he provided a novel addition to revolutionary theory by moving beyond the Leninist or Maoist conception of party control.

In fact, Fanon wished to empower the most downtrodden and forgotten. Also, the colonizer—the West—had to be completely removed, although he was counting on foreign assistance based on the fear of what might otherwise happen. By deporting the Westerners, Fanon imagined a revolution made for the most excluded who must exercise sovereignty and power themselves. *Black Skin, White Masks* shows his view was that race further alienated colonized from colonizer. Part of the wide appeal of *The Wretched of the Earth* lay in its powerful writing and rhetoric. Moreover, it matched up with a more populist opposition to a centralized party, at least in Western Europe and North America. Fanon also strongly expressed the anti-Western sentiment against the colonizers.

Nonetheless, is Fanon related to Marxism? Where Marx emphasized the oppression by a class, Fanon focused primarily on the fact that the oppression (which notably included psychological oppression) came from a colonizer, who only secondarily was a member of the bourgeoisie. The most active force of resistance was not the proletariat; and Fanon criticized the Leninist-style party. While mainly addressing the very problems Marx had outlined and using in a contrary or oblique way many Marxist categories, Fanon proposed different, sometimes opposite answers. Yet in the grand scheme of things, he still looked toward the goal of socialism; Fanon might argue that he simply provided a better means and goal. After all, he had not been the first to make revisions. Indeed, like his Marxist predecessors throughout the world, Fanon could aver that he was devising a reformulated Marxism that would better fit the decolonizing world.

Including Fanon among the Marxists reveals both continuity and a continuing suppleness of this revolutionary theory, especially as it became a key influence on the revolutionary ideas of anticolonialism. Such constant revisions (even without Fanon's) call into question Marx's own thesis whose end promised human freedom. To recapitulate, Marx predicted that the precise stages of development—the apotheosis of bourgeois development coupled to the class consciousness of the proletariat—would provide the violent revolution and speedy transition to a better world. Various reconfigurations of class conflict and Party involvement might disrupt the emergence, or at least confidence in the immediate arrival, of that utopian socialist society predicted by Marx. But his successors—Lenin, Mao, Debray, and others—changed the shock troops in the class struggle against the bourgeoisie to include a major role for peasants. This transformation neglected the economic underpinning of Marxism that made the revolution coincide with an enormous expansion of industrial production. Thus, the immanent revolution no longer would bring sufficient material goods to free individuals from toil. With this logic removed, the revolution would lose its inevitable positive ending, as the cause and salvation of the revolution were meant to be high industrial productivity. One might additionally suggest that sacrifices to a long-term change, to be engineered by a "dictatorship" of either proletariat or party, might become more difficult to justify. Revisions may, thus, have enabled revolution in colonized societies, but they also undermined Marxist economic assumptions. Such ideological innovations undercut the theory's prediction that Communism would lead to a utopian end. As such, the end could not be used so easily to justify the means and the right to claim sovereignty on behalf of the working class.

Nonetheless, Marx and his followers, near and distant, dominated revolutionary activity for most of the twentieth century up to the 1989 collapse of communism in the Soviet bloc. Marxism's enormous appeal surely related in part to the promise of the *Communist Manifesto* and its utopian ending as well as the elasticity and adaptability of the theory. While these two features seem to contradict one another, the advantages are also many, especially the relevance to the economic aspirations of many countries. They are hardly the only reason for the amazing endurance and penetration of the theory. One of the most important has been the reaction to change by leading Western powers in the last century. Especially since the Second World War, but even before, these nations were willing to ignore or even support those who campaigned for liberalism, nationalism, and democracy. Revolutionary violence proved unnecessary. However, interference and resistance met those who demanded deep structural changes, which often were already associated with Marxism. This hostility pushed radicals more to embrace the Marxist association, in order to receive support from Russia, China, and elsewhere, the only road open to them. The bipolar Cold War rendered this tendency more evident. Its end, combined with the great retreat of communism in 1989, has in fact reduced the selection of Marxism as a popular label.

> What suggestions might the Cuban and Vietnamese revolutionaries have for Frantz Fanon?

Revolutionary religion

Although anticolonialism also enormously stimulated revolution in the Middle East, it was not the only motivation for change. In fact, after the Second World War, many issues affected this region, including new religious movements and responses to the creation of Israel. While the roots of resistance to imperialism lay in the late nineteenth century, countries in this region were still freeing themselves from European imperialism. Countries from Morocco to Pakistan broke from European rule in the years after the Second World War, though many had repressive monarchs or military leaders, who ruled with Western support and interference. These nations' strategic and economic value (oil reserves in particular) had drawn extraordinary interest. Further, by consolidating and extending Jewish holdings in Palestine, the creation of the state of Israel inspired various degrees of anxiety about Western overreach. Long-term hostility toward Jews only exacerbated problems. In sum, a string of repressive regimes had mainly replaced colonialism, though there were exceptions like the republic of Lebanon.

This situation, which left Middle Easterners often unsatisfied with their governments, inspired the desire for popular change. The first major revolutionary alteration in this system occurred in Iran where a religiously inspired action in 1978 led to a theologically run Islamic state. Although the leaders of this movement imagined a country based on traditional values, they also wrought a revolution in many aspects of life. This was not the only major uprising during the next several decades. The world watched with incredible amazement and excitement when in 2009, starting in Tunisia and extending around the southern and eastern Mediterranean Sea, the "Arab Spring" began to topple authoritarian regimes and institute democracies. The outcome of these upheavals remains very uncertain. Radical religious movements have also influenced all of these Arab societies, including a powerful fundamentalist movement. Somewhat ideologically connected to or stimulated by the revolution in Iran, it has sought to transform Islamic lands into traditional religious states. Often the fundamentalists advanced their goals by terrorism addressed toward the West whose presence and influence had to be purged from their lands to achieve religious goals. Most famous in a movement with many branches and viewpoints—often contradictory one to another—was Al-Qaeda and more recently the Islamic State, both of which may be viewed as extremist religious additions to the long, post-1945 history of anti-Western and anticolonial political movements. Some may reasonably object that these groups' heavy and direct use of terrorism makes any relationship very tentative.

The focus here is on the Iranian revolution because it expressed new revolutionary ideas. Revolutionaries of the Arab Spring also created a new mix but primarily a mélange of liberalism and democracy. Other groups in this later revolutionary surge sought to increase religion's role in politics. Nevertheless, freedom and democracy remained in play across the region, even as these were diluted by being applied more and more broadly across a political coalition with widely varying beliefs.

Iran was never formally colonized by Europeans, but it had been under enormous pressures from Great Britain and Russia which competed there for influence. Taking advantage of political instability after the First World War, Rezi Shah engineered a coup d'état and assumed the throne in 1921. His family (the Pahlavis) ruled on and off until 1979, when a popular uprising brought the Ayatollah Ruhollah Khomeini to power. While over time, the Pahlavis had modernized the country along Western lines, many forces combined to unseat Mohammad Reza Shah Pahlavi. His indifference to bazaar merchants and favoritism to foreign investors and big business cost him serious support with the Iranian populace. He accomplished little toward land reform, and this alienated farmers. And in a religious country, he was a modernizer who favored feminism and Western mores more than the traditional could accept. Also, his reliance on the United States proved unpopular. Finally, an economic slump in the 1970s exacerbated all those concerns.

Meanwhile, Khomeini, having been exiled, continued to attack the Shah's policies and offered in contrast an anti-Western spiritual culture based in Islam. In the mosques, disquiet with the current regime grew along with Khomeini's popularity and support. The general public deserted the Shah, and so did the army which refused to repress demonstrations. In February 1979, Pahlavi fled the country and died the following year. Khomeini returned to a tumultuous welcome and a revolutionary mandate. He shortly began to institute a religious state.

One-third of the way through his exile for challenging the Iranian government, Khomeini had delivered a series of speeches which many regard as his best known work and which appeared in 1970 as a selection called "Islamic Government."[18] It provides a comprehensive idea of Khomeini's overall political philosophy when he was still several years away from a triumphant return. Like the writings of many revolutionaries, the book bursts with energy—but lacks order, returning over and again to the same themes, and exploring them in slightly different ways. Still this work reveals the cleric's viewpoint before the practical politics of 1979 altered his approach.

Khomeini clearly outlined a very straightforward principle of governing: the religious state. "Islamic Government" repeatedly defines the basic outline, perhaps no more successfully than in the following paragraph:

> The commands of the Most Noble Messenger (upon whom be peace and blessings) are those that he himself issued in the course of exercising his governmental function, as when, for example, he commanded the Muslims to follow the army of Usama, to protect the frontiers of the Islamic state in a certain way, to levy taxes on certain categories of people, and in general to interact with people in certain prescribed ways. All of these were commands of the Prophet .... God Almighty has commanded us to follow the Messenger and the holders of authority, our obeying them is actually an expression of obedience to God.[19]

In this vital passage, Khomeini laid out the need for continued subservience to Islamic traditions in the present as in the past. God demanded religious obedience, and Khomeini's plea was for a complete reaffirmation of the initial system.

In addition to restoring the past, an ambitious goal likely more expansive than even those of Lenin and Mao, Khomeini noted specific aspects of that past: a regime in which the statements of Mohammed ("most noble messenger") are validated as commands from God. Throughout the rest of the work, Khomeini discussed the continuing authority passed down through subsequent leaders [Imams] which for the present was the same as that of the Prophet. In fact, Khomeini elsewhere in the text affirmed that no legislature would be required, only an administration and judiciary to enforce the laws already given. Religion and the law proved to be one and the same.

And that law was Sharia. Anticipating that many believed Sharia to be harsh, Khomeini vigorously defended it. In part, he compared Western justice with that of the Qu'ran by noting the very long prison sentences imposed on drug offenses compared with lighter sentences for alcohol consumption in Muslim countries. Khomeini insisted that another advantage of Sharia was fairness as a jurist could not go beyond the specified law. Nonetheless, many Muslims might not have used the example of stoning as a just punishment for fornication that Khomeini deemed acceptable, indicating that it fits the crime.

Khomeini bitterly attacked those responsible for thwarting the institution of Islamic government and often charged both the Israelis and the Jews as well as the British and Americans: "Can you not see the danger? Do you not see that the Israelis are attacking, killing, and destroying and the British are helping them? You sit there watching but you must wake up; you must try to find a remedy for the ills of the people."[20] Also vile were the Western puppets, the vices of sex, usury common in the West, and the material corruption of Islamic leaders. "Islamic Government" charted the history of these problems and began with the anti-Islamic propaganda that Khomeini asserted that Jews had created at the beginning of Islam. For the last 300 years imperialists had sought to stamp out the faith. Even back during the Crusades, European invaders thought that the main threat to their political and economic power was Islam. These foreigners, he explained, sought to destroy faith by denigrating it as empty of principle and advice for everyday living and consumed by meaningless ritual. By such misinformation, they sought to deny Islam its "vital, revolutionary aspect and to prevent Muslims from arousing themselves in order to gain their freedom ... and create a government that will assure their happiness and allow them to live lives worthy of human beings."[21] Further, the Ottomans who had not been all that faithful to Islam had to be destroyed, their territory broken into pieces, to assure the end of Western domination.

To redress these problems, Khomeini insisted that Muslims, led by the Imams and the *faqih* (judges), should act: "Whatever is needed to preserve national independence and liberty is again precisely what the *faqih* have to offer." These men would not surrender to foreign influences and would defend national rights and "the freedom, independence, and territorial integrity of the Islamic homeland." Khomeini repeatedly declared that a struggle might be necessary. Elsewhere, he noted, without clarifying whether he meant simply to enforce the laws or go beyond them: "It is our duty to preserve Islam—this duty is one of the most important obligations incumbent upon us; it is more necessary than prayer and fasting. It is for the sake of fulfilling this duty that blood must sometimes be shed."[22] Elsewhere this treatise singled out for praise those who had valiantly resisted tyrants and who wished to "fill with earth the mouths of those who praise them."[23] He also noted that other tyrants had previously been killed for their oppression. And this work ended with the fervent hope that all people would struggle to free Islamic countries from the "vile agents" of imperialism and then secure these countries' liberty.[24] To be sure, Khomeini generally avoided describing the physical destruction of such countries and relied on the term struggle which could be nonviolent. Yet it is difficult to read his repeated references to such confrontations and not imagine that he expected violence.

Thus, Khomeini desired to establish an Islamic theocracy whose government would enforce Sharia law ... But where? Although he occasionally seemed to be speaking only of Iran with references to the Shah and other specific circumstances, the plan and language are general enough to suggest that he hoped for a full rising of

Muslims to obtain a unified government over their own territories. Khomeini noted that formerly the Shi'a had laid claim to the entire caliphate ruled by an Islamic government. According to tradition, one Imam had mapped out the entire Islamic area and then declared to the oppressors: "Everything within these boundaries is our legitimate state. We should rule over it, and you are usurpers."[25] Khomeini sought to persuade his readers that such claims could be realized in the present. Reassuring Muslim rulers that true believers would be left in place, he averred that it was time for a great state. Noting that there were 700 million Muslims in the world, including 170 million Shi'a, Khomeini urged them to move forward. All that was required were rulers with sufficient resolve.[26] Here also violence was strongly implied. The language of the book repeatedly insinuated this vision and seldom distinguished countries while speaking generally of Islam.

In sum, Khomeini, while out of power, urged the creation of a fundamentalist theological state to be defended and expanded, by violence, if necessary. Although a blueprint for a jihad, it was not, by the definition used in this study, a revolution. Even though its makers conceived it as one, it lacked a progressive political or social agenda and in fact paid considerable attention to a reaffirmation of past glory and practice. Progress was not to be made by innovation but by restoration. Khomeini specifically stated these changes would be a return. Of course, this treatise suggested substantial assistance for the poor, but this too lay within Islamic traditions. Khomeini firmly believed in a tradition of private property and the stoic acceptance of poverty. However, here in Iran as during other such moments—beginning in America and France—the definition of revolution evolved.

Scholars, particularly Ervand Abrahamian, have argued that after 1970, Khomeini's politics began to expand beyond religious principles.[27] Perhaps he wished to position himself better to attract the populace and a wider group of workers rather than favor those with significant private property. Other observers interpret this change as a bow to the inevitable because even the monarchy had opened up some opportunities to poor and had permitted wider political participation. Or it may be that Khomeini and others came into contact with more radical ideas, including those in *The Wretched of the Earth*, which had been translated.

Whatever the causes, the new constitution enacted during the first months of the Revolution of 1979 reflected significant political change beyond the vision in the treatise "Islamic State." While the caliphate belonged to all Muslims, the revolution evidently sought to invest sovereignty only in those coreligionists inside the borders. Comparing it with Khomeini's early political imaginings—an Islamic leader, no legislature, an administration, and a judiciary—one detects a dramatic change. To be certain, the Constitution made Iran an Islamic country headed by a leader named by the Assembly of Experts, who themselves were elected in an environment likely to be dominated by the religious. Given immense authority, the leader was considered to be "equal with the rest of the people." In sum, the political weight of the leader balanced that of the rest of the population. Moreover, appointed by the leader was the Council of Guardians that evaluated every legislative bill according to the principles of Sharia.

Despite the potentially overwhelming power of the leader—amplified by a large number of appointments at his discretion—political rights in the society far exceeded what Khomeini had been considering just one year earlier. Ethnic groups and women received equal rights. This new constitution included some juries and forbade torture to extract information but did not eliminate it entirely. While one could hold any belief one wished, one could not publish it, if it "were detrimental to the fundamental principles of Islam or the rights of the public."

More important, a legislature with significant powers was created. Its 270 members could "establish laws on all matters" and could not be prosecuted for their opinions in performing their duties. Yet every bill had to be approved by the Council of Guardians for its compatibility with Islam. Although the Ayatollah's movement had insisted that no need existed for a parliament, one was established, and its wide policy swings in subsequent years indicated that it was far from powerless.

Perhaps the relative restraint of those occupying the position of Leader ultimately determined the structure of government, but a kind of functioning democracy did emerge. Or, as noted above, the government needed support from a public that had experienced some democracy under the Shah, and this past predicated democratic and judicial procedures beyond religious tradition. In these circumstances, significant social programs were elaborated, but these actions were more tentative and subject to reversal by political and juridical officials. Nonetheless, some of the same political influences likely caused the emergence of social and economic policies.

Relating to social programs were conceptions of society that too were being rethought. Khomeini had argued previous to the revolution in Iran that the rich and the poor had a role to fill. In fact, very much as had Old Regime Europe, the cleric saw society as a "multilayered hierarchy" with peasants and laborers at the bottom and the landlords and clerics at the top. Dependent on one another, each needed to respect the other. All was divinely ordered, making any change extremely problematic. This rigid system included slavery. At the bottom were infidels (Jews, Christians, etc.) who were roughly equivalent to the "untouchables" of India.

In the 1970s and 1980s, however, Khomeini shifted his view: society consisted of the oppressors and the oppressed. In this system the upper class consisted of the wealthy, the corrupt, the lazy, and other undesirables. The oppressed, as well as the hungry and unemployed, hailed from the slums. Given this dialectic, good naturally resided on the side of the oppressed. Their oppressors flouted Islam and supported the Shah and Americans. In such circumstances the poor respected private property, but the rich abused it. Khomeini supported policies of redistribution and promised an "Islamic utopia free of injustice, inequality, poverty, social conflict, unemployment, landlessness, foreign dependence, imperial exploitation, political oppression, social alienation, prostitution, alcoholism, drug addiction, crime, nepotism, government corruption, and bureaucratic red tape."[28] And indeed, increasingly, Khomeini himself was identified as a man of the people, living modestly and frugally.[29]

As events evolved, their progressive nature changed Khomeini's initial goal of instituting Sharia to create a movement whose overall footprint must be seen as revolutionary, regardless of its origins in a conservative religious revival of the past. As such, the Iranian revolution ranks among the most novel of events. It also signaled a new chapter in the history of the idea of revolution and revealed its continued renewal, for better or worse, as a mode of human political expression. To be sure, progressive policies in Iran have waxed and waned since 1979 but have remained at least somewhat vital. Whether the current rise in religious movements throughout the Middle East and beyond will remain atavistic and reactionary or will join the list of revolutions remains to be seen. If the latter, it opens the door to the study of such efforts as revolutionary. Truly different from most modern conservatives who tend not to seek change at all, these traditionalists used revolutions to achieve a variety of results—an unstable confection of change and reactionary goals. Ultimately, what other Islamists decide to do as they mobilize remains uncertain—pure or revised Sharia?

The era of decolonization thus added new features to the idea of revolution: critiques of Western colonialism, more emphasis on the debilitating effects of racism in economic and political life (as well as personal psychology), revisions of Leninist ideas about the role of revolutionary parties, and the importance of religious traditions. Indeed, religion now gained the mobilizing power that Marxism earlier had held, in part because religion could be fused into an anti-Western view and used to conceptualize alternative systems of political organization.

Among all these revolutionaries, do you see any consistent topics for their complaints?

Essay 4

The Other in Revolution

Although this book has generally focused on what revolutionaries favored, it is worth noting what they opposed. Indeed, revolutionaries were almost required to specify, and usually vilify, the opposition in order to justify the violent action contemplated. Consequently, the Declaration of Independence spent more time on the crimes of George III than on revolutionary goals; the French revolutionaries, in the debate about the execution of Louis XVI, concentrated not only on his actions but on his fundamental symbolic hostility to the revolution; and Fanon attacked imperialists in part because their existence in and of itself had to be given up to free the Algerians. This is not to say that revolutionaries were right or wrong in the necessity of this approach, but generally Ford does not attack General Motors to get customers to buy their cars.

Furthermore, other more subtle negative themes emerged, including attacks on the spouse of the ruler. Venturing outside the expected domestic sphere could expose women to venomous attacks like those for Alexandra, wife of the Tsar during the Russian Revolution. Even normal political contests could use odious treatment and insinuations for Argentina's Eva Perón (which continues in the musical *Evita*) as well as attacks on Hillary Clinton's sexuality. But no spouse has ever been treated as Marie-Antoinette was: critiques that certainly contributed to her execution. Although Marie-Antoinette had tried to chart a more assertive course for her husband and was involved in plots and plans, she was attacked as licentious, even to the point of accusations of sexual abuse of her son and incest with her brother-in-law and of lesbian relationships with friends. Also, she was portrayed as simply greedy and conniving.

Why did revolutionaries mount such attacks on spouses? Of course, a family that included such a person must be corrupt, as Marie-Antoinette seemed to be, most infamously, in the Diamond Necklace affair, which seemed to inculpate her as a greedy woman. But she, along with other wives, was accused of not following proper behavior, which embarrassed her husband. More than that, in a patriarchal world, husbands were supposed to control their wives. Those who could not appeared emasculated, not man enough to be a husband—or more relevantly, a national leader. Revolutionaries could reach their target by attacking the wives.

Symbols could also be used to establish a difference and undermine the opposition. Simply establishing difference could create an attack. Philosopher Mircea Eliade long ago wrote that one way or another humans, whether secular or religious, stretched to connect earth to the heavens to relate the mundane life of man to something far greater. Christians under the Catholic Bourbon monarchy believed this "axis mundi" stretched from man through French Church, headed by the king, to God. The Gothic and Romanesque towers of Paris, Chartres, and elsewhere were a physical manifestation of this connection. In the revolution based on "natural law" embedded by God, the axis was represented by the liberty tree generally and during the Jacobin dictatorship a mountain. Nature had replaced the divine. Such changes distanced the revolutionaries from the Church, discredited in this era while still remaining divine. American revolutionaries made another symbolic gesture. In opposition to the redcoats, the British military that fired on unarmed civilians in Boston and who were regimented, uniformed oppressors, the colonists described their own soldiers as hardy volunteers, commoners, fighting smartly, and providing the "shot heard round the world." Such rhetorical devices characterized the democracy in opposition to the despotism and rigidity of monarchy. Revolutionaries needed to create and occupy the symbolic "high" ground.

In the twentieth century, attire especially proved to be another good indirect method for making statements that could position the revolutionaries as they wished to attack their opposition. While Chiang Kaishek appears as a military martinet, Mao dressed casually, seemingly like a peasant. Of course, his garb was as studied as his opponent, but to the revolutionary's advantage, provided a much more agreeable set of associations. Compared to Chiang in a military dress uniform, Mao seemed like a regular guy, unconcerned with his appearance. Mao's fashion statement was positive enough that worldwide his dress was copied and sold along with the Nehru jacket of the Indian leader and Gandhi associate. Both gave off the aura of the relaxed leader. Although the Cuban president and dictator Fulgencio Batista often wore a business suit, he too could don a military-style uniform. How could he compete in approachability with the relaxed Castro who most often appeared in fatigues and his colleague Che whose long hair

FIGURE 4.1 *Chinese general Chiang Kaishek. (Photo by Popperfoto/Getty Images.)*

FIGURE 4.2 *Chinese children in uniform in front of a picture of Chairman Mao Zedong (1893–1976) during China's Cultural Revolution. (Photo by Hulton Archive/Getty Images.)*

and uncommon good looks made his face familiar on posters in American dormitories.

To a certain extent, these Latin Americans descended, in terms of image, from the redshirted Italian nationalist Giuseppe Garibaldi and the unkempt, long-haired Karl Marx. Another style in contrast to overdressed and overstuffed European colonists and imperialists was by the simple garb adopted by Ho Chi Minh and Mohandas Gandhi. Not only could clothing communicate a proper

FIGURE 4.3 *Jawaharlal Nehru, the newly elected President of the All India Congress, talking with Mahatma Gandhi, Indian political leader, at a meeting of the Congress, Bombay, India, July 15, 1946. (Photo by Underwood Archives/Getty Images.)*

connection to the populace, it could define the revolutionary as more manly. Avoiding heavily decorated uniforms in favor of spartan dress spoke to a revolutionary edge in masculinity. Revolutionary spouses reflected this stylistic differentiation by adopting simple clothing as well. Some "revolutionary" attire was invented, some traditional, often it worked well in creating positive opinions.

Feminists have often had a difficult time in political revolutions. What parts of these political ideologies have worked to the advantage or to the disadvantage of women?

FIGURE 4.4 *Col. Fulgencio Batista. (Photo by Thomas D. Mcavoy/The LIFE Picture Collection/Getty Images.)*

FIGURE 4.5 *Cuban revolutionary Fidel Castro during an address in Cuba after Batista was forced to flee. (Photo by Keystone/Getty Images.)*

FIGURE 4.6 *Argentinian-born Cuban Communist revolutionary leader Ernesto Che Guevara (1928–1967). (Photo by Keystone/Getty Images.)*

Further Reading

Abrahamian, Ervand. *Khomeinism: Essays on the Islamic Republic.* Berkeley, 1993.

Bakhash, Shaul. *The Reign of the Ayatollahs: Iran and the Islamic Revolution.* New York, 1984.

Betts, Raymond F. *Decolonization*, 2nd Ed. New York and London, 1998.

Chamberlain, M.E. *Decolonization: The Fall of the European Empires*, 2nd Ed. London, 1999.

Daniels, Robert V. *Year of the Heroic Guerrilla: World Revolution and Counterrevolution in 1968.* New York, 1989.

Duara, Prasenjit. Ed. *Decolonization: Perspectives from Now and Then.* London and New York, 2004.

Duiker, William J. *The Communist Road to Power in Vietnam.* Boulder, CO, 1981.

Duiker, William J. *Ho Chi Minh.* New York, 2000.

Holland, R.F. *European Decolonization, 1918–1981: An Introductory Survey.* New York, 1985.

Khánh, Huynh Kim. *Vietnamese Communism, 1925–1945.* Ithaca and London, 1982.

Macey, David. *Frantz Fanon: A Biography*, 2nd Ed. London, 2012.

Ruiz, Ramon Eduardo. *Cuba: The Making of a Revolution.* Amherst, 1968.

Szulc, Tad. *Fidel: A Critical Portrait.* New York, 1986.

Trager, Frank N. Ed. *Marxism in Southeast Asia: A Study of Four Countries.* Stanford, 1959.

Turner, Robert F. *Vietnamese Communism: Its Origins and Development.* Stanford, 1975.

Conclusion: Further Reflections

With the American Revolution, political revolutions began to occur rather unexpectedly for contemporaries. Despite two events in England called revolutions, the practice had lapsed and eighteenth-century activists related only to one—the Glorious Revolution of 1688, which had in fact been a restoration. As Keith Baker has so clearly shown, the term in the French language did not have its modern meaning in the eighteenth century,[1] until its definition evolved to reflect the radical changes in North America and France.

A new age began with the Declaration of Independence's clarion call that men held inalienable rights including legal equality. By the time Jefferson penned these words, the Americans had every reason to believe that they would have to fight for them. In fitting these words and revolution to violence, the definition shifted. Activities almost fifteen years later in France confirmed his novel meaning. Two new things had been created or at least re-created: the notion of radical change accompanied by action.

This book shows the malleability of the notion of revolution in supporting fundamentally different events over the last 250 years. Not only did the ideas change, but the propagation of these ideas began to link doctrines together, including notions of revolution and violence that became key parts of the strategies of Marxist, nationalist, and religious revolutionaries. This trajectory continues, even as these words are written.

Although everyone knows much of the story of revolutionary ideas, they do not know it in much detail or in its evolution. Neither the novelty nor the details are particularly clear. Even those who know Marx seldom know how his successors related and innovated. And the passion and consistent need of most revolutionary leaders to marshal ideas as well as the passion of movement discussions prove surprising. In brief, this book arrayed revolutions in four chronological layers: political liberties and legal equality; national liberation, and economic and social equality; the adoption of Marx to underdeveloped Russia and China; and finally, the use of old ingredients and the new ones of religion and anti-Western sentiments to focus on the peasants and colonized people. Evolving notions about who might claim sovereignty justified seizure of power from one kind of regime to another. Future studies can build on and examine themes that have arisen in connection with the primary focus on revolutionary ideology: the gap that rather predictably emerged between revolutionary principles and performance as well as the idealism of many revolutionaries. Also evident is their potentially problematic adaptation to circumstances. The impact of these revolutions remains difficult to measure because of the inability to know what would have happened had they not occurred. Other areas, some just touched on in this work, include: the overwhelming role of Marxists; the post–Second World War resistance from the West to revolutions; and the interplay of intellectuals and activists in revolution.

Scholars, studying the general history of revolution, have seldom narrated either the long-term chronological continuities or changes of ideologies. Instead, as discussed below, they have had other interests that the focus of this book may benefit. Most scholars of broad revolutionary phenomena—mainly sociologists and political scientists—have considered revolutions collectively, to generalize about the outbreak, function, and reasons for failure.[2] With these disciplinary approaches, not surprisingly the initial effort to understand revolution placed social and economic factors at the heart of the mechanism of those political changes. The first generation of researchers focused on iconic revolutions like the French, Russian, and Chinese and examined social instability, economic frustrations, and group rivalries. Such scholars concurred that once society was roiled, simply an incident or an error would tip matters into revolution. As Jack Goldstone has pointed out, the variables developed often were too vague to adequately assess and provided only suggestive results.

By the late 1970s a new cohort with a similar perspective had entered the field and adumbrated new subjects for review; but most of all these younger scholars wanted to transform the search for causes by adding a precision that would allow for prediction. Perhaps the best known of these were Theda Skocpol. In *States and Social Revolutions: A Comparative Analysis of France, Russia, and China*, Skocpol argued that social revolutions could emerge only in societies in which an organized government ruled over an agrarian society.[3] She pointed to the frailty of the structure of such countries as a potential rift existed between a modern government and a large peasantry isolated in the countryside. To take just one part of her argument, one might say that she clearly saw the fault line and posited that when the eruption came, most important was the economic strength or weakness of the cities. Thus, during the French Revolution in which large holdings were rare, economic Jacobinism, with an emphasis on a wide distribution of small properties, won out. Conversely, Russia's burgeoning industry provided a base whose resources provided the Bolsheviks with the margin necessary to create a socialist country.

Following Skocpol and others, an avalanche of scholars argued that the definition of revolution must be broadened to include uprisings in which change came from mass mobilization. This expanded the field but also included so many events that it became impossible to isolate a few cases. Spreading across an even larger area of inquiry than before, the field began to abandon universal explanations to make mid-level abstract generalizations about how a revolution could work. Once again, Goldstone made a signal contribution by isolating two axes of research—the impact of the international systems and the interaction of government, elites, and the populace. For example, one very promising area of research concerned the nature of the elite. Scholars have posited that if elites are highly divided, a strong government can resist. In the opposite circumstance, a revolution becomes more likely.

The more recent wave of scholarship has produced numerous studies from different perspectives that endeavor to ask general questions about revolutions and then at least offer partial answers or suggested hypotheses that analyze gender as well as group and individual motivation to join or resist. Approaches such as rational choice and quantification have blended the case study with broader data.

But in the midst of this eclectic outburst of theories, findings, and new topics, two areas stand out—leadership and ideology—where this study may contribute. Recent scholarship has, for example, focused on the relationship between revolutionary ideology and social acceptance of the revolutionary movement. While acknowledging that the ideology of the leadership and ideological explanations available to the "masses" often differ, one should note that revolutionaries within their movements debated theory with passion and clearly a desire to convince one another. The emphasis on goals and beliefs evident in this volume may provide additional questions for the agenda of other social scientists. Essentially the revolutionaries' views—their substance, logic, and passion as well as their use of evidence and rhetoric—constituted behavior that inflected their actions and, in many cases, the events in which they participated. Even their frequent revisions, which were often pragmatic, surely sometimes even cynical, adjustments, indicated that they believed that they needed to convince at least some colleagues or elements in the population. A true cynic, living among cynics, would not have needed to address a change in posture—at least not when communicating to peers. Clearly, revolutionary theory served insiders as the opportunity to maintain solidarity as well as an occasion to splinter. Case studies about cohesion and breakup should allow scholars to understand better what engendered effectiveness. And of course, such a study should consider leadership as well as intellectual debate. Lenin and Robespierre were compelling writers; and they were much more forgiving toward allies and ruthless toward enemies. In dreadful situations they prevailed—but in the Frenchman's case only for a while. His execution and likewise Lenin's early death deprive us of comparisons to many long-lived revolutionaries.

Despite the new emphasis among social scientists on ideals and leadership, this remains a minor subject in their ranks. Very few works, more discursive in nature, either examine or even comment over the long term on revolutionary ideas. Nonetheless, three scholarly books, all of which made a big intellectual splash when published, are worthy of considering in regard to their notions about revolutionary belief. The authors are Jacob Talmon, James Billington, and Francis Fukuyama. Each book inspired significant contemporary discussion and debate as opinions were revised and rethought. But it was the originality of the arguments that made these books so well known, and it is these we must examine.

Among the most controversial books ever written on revolution was Jacob Talmon's *The Origins of Totalitarian Democracy*.[4] Published in 1952 at the height of the Cold War, this book—a conservative attack on liberalism as well as Marxism—argued that the Enlightenment held within it the seeds of totalitarian government. Brilliant and persuasive, Talmon sought to demonstrate that elements of this eighteenth-century philosophe's version of liberty could end up as dictatorship. Not only did the Enlightenment promise liberty, it also sought equality. People must be blended into one nation; those who protested this condition were iniquitous, hostile to the general good. Disagreement was antisocial. Talmon believed that this twisting of liberty and dissent into oppression began with the French Revolution and Robespierre, who used revolutionary dictatorship and its muscle to exclude dissenters. Property too had to be made equal; and though the Jacobins were ambivalent on this, Babeuf provided communism as the logical conclusion to the oppressive inclination. And from all this followed the Marxist regimes that were ascendant when Talmon wrote his book.

Despite the significant reaction this work received, by the 1980s the work had faded in scholarly circles until François Furet and his colleagues provided a tempered but still potent version of this argument—a controversy that still demarcates the scholarly difference between left and right today.[5] Perhaps the most powerful defense of the Enlightenment is Talmon's own assertion at the very beginning of his book that the Enlightenment also possessed an individualistic logic. But he then, seemingly contradictorily, described an inexorable march toward totalitarianism. Apparently, a series of events intervened, rather than an ineluctable track to tyranny. Talmon in his conclusion again noted that humanity was not condemned to totalitarianism. Indeed, after the violence of the Paris Commune in 1870, resentment allowed some individualist regimes to remain, based as he believed in a "history and nature" that required humans to be pragmatic and accept inequality as a reality.

Whatever the politics of Talmon's book, it illuminated the ideas of revolution which most social scientists do not. So the argument here benefits from Talmon's emphasis, even as it does not support the general drift of his work. Even Marxism did not conform to the rigidity that Talmon implied. After all, Marx himself believed that an industrial regime previously unimaginable would create "freedom" for everyone.

This is not to deny that many, if not all, Marxist regimes suppressed liberty, even in some periods backed by harsh regimes of incarceration and terror. Yet Talmon offers no evidence at all beyond Babeuf that the resemblance of such regimes revealed a connected logic and politics. And evidently, from the existence of many non-Marxist dictatorships over the last two centuries, the Marxists did not have a monopoly on sheer lust for power without any feints toward humanity or a desire for order. In the end, scholars have mainly agreed about the repressive nature of Marxist societies but have not concurred about a deterministic line drawn from the eighteenth century through the next 200 years to Lenin, Stalin, Mao, and others.

This book backs the hesitations of other scholars, particularly by its emphasis on the layered expansion and change of revolutionary ideas. In fact, the dense activity visible in each era—especially the intellectual life, the development of ideas, the planning, and the revolution—provides the framework in which conspirators operated. When borrowing ideas from predecessors, they converted them, matching them to their own needs and circumstances. So, in particular when Lenin referred to Robespierre and found inspiration in the Jacobin, he still learned and adapted from his own deep well of needs and experience. Moreover, in the case of the Bolsheviks, almost certainly they were equally or more aware of the Communards of 1870 Paris, and to a lesser extent the revolutionaries of 1848. A second but related reason to disconnect direct language linkages from one era to another is that revolutionaries were always dealing with one issue, significantly beyond their control—the counter to their revolution. By definition, revolutions always have grave opposition that leads to violent conflict, because without it, they are a reform movement. And in particular, the opposition was fundamentally different for Lenin than for Robespierre. Lifting the idea straight from his predecessors would not have been very likely as Lenin was, of course, required to consider the method to achieve the result desired.

James Billington's *Fire in the Minds of Men* (1980)[6] posited that revolutionaries shared a conviction, but rather than intellectual, it was psychological. Before discussing this thesis, credit must be given to this enormous tome (677 pages of text and notes) for its excellent chronicle of revolutionary ideas. Billington endeavored to provide the entire sweep of revolutionary ideas from the French to the Russian revolution and covered not just the successful revolutionaries but all those who innovated toward that goal. In fact, his greatest contribution was placing the French Revolution, nationalism, Marx, and the Russian heirs in an orderly chronology of radical thinkers. The focus and depth of coverage make this an unparalleled survey of such thought.

Yet for all that, Billington failed to prove his thesis, partly from extraordinary inattention. The title provocatively announced his general view that revolutionary ideas exist beyond reason, acting as a combustible material that cannot be extinguished. Beginning not with the Enlightenment but the secret Masonic ideals and lasting at least through the Russian Revolution, revolution emerged as a faith, in fact a surrogate for religious belief. The author announced that he first wrote "to linger on the mystery and the majesty of faith itself," and continued:

> The heart of revolutionary faith, like any faith, is fire: ordinary material transformed into extraordinary form, quantities of warmth suddenly changing the quality of substance. If we do not know what fire is, we know what it does. It burns. It destroys life; but it also supports it as a source of heat, light, and—above all—fascination.[7]

This faith originated in secret societies, particularly German ones. Billington singled out the Illuminati, a secret society growing up in Bavaria in 1776. Perceiving the world as a battle between light and darkness, the group sought to advance the former. Central to this group was the cult of fire. Promoting its organization and coopting the Masons, the Illuminati and its ideas gained a strong foothold and endowed most of the early revolutions with a burning desire to defeat evil. The key here, it seems to me, was the passion behind the movement, rather than its specific approach to changing the world.

After establishing the thesis (sparsely treating the American Revolution and apparently excusing it as well), Billington, as he noted in his introduction, did not return to it. Instead, he assiduously explored a succession of revolutionary beliefs as they developed in Europe.

Like Talmon, Billington believed revolution a runaway project, but instead of focusing on ideas, he concentrated on emotions. Nonetheless, he established in the course of his book that the revolutionaries were far more dogged and determined than mystical. Certainly they had a faith, but they were consumed with the details. After all, Lenin had to wait some twenty years for a revolution that could not erupt through a burst of light but came from taking advantage of "objective" conditions that he ended up responding to but still regarded as arriving outside his wish or command. And, as noted above, why would Lenin pay so much attention to the changing details of his writings, if they were at most a means of conversion and indoctrination into a magical order. Lenin was a strategist of action. If revolutionaries might be rightfully accused of passion, they were guilty of a certainty about their goal and a commitment to doing whatever was necessary to achieve it. This often involved ruthlessness and many deaths as well as significant calculation. They did not perceive their commitment as an inner light but rather a pragmatic good with "real" advantages. They had lots of work to do—even of the most disagreeable and inhumane sort. In short, with far more evidence than Talmon, Billington mightily chronicled radical efforts but he did far less to convince that the revolutionaries went amiss because of their passionate conspiracy. Perhaps the religious revolutionaries seem more congruent with this argument than the secular ones. Yet commitment to a cause and passionate emotions seems quite different; the first lacks the quality of irrationality that the second requires.

Although Francis Fukuyama's *The End of History and the Last Man*[8] received from the left a rough reception at its publication for its antirevolution stance, his theory is different than those of Talmon and Billington, for he praised the liberal and democratic revolutions. In fact, Fukuyama viewed the emergence of liberal democracies as the dominant form of government as a trend highly likely to continue. He implied but did not develop an explanation of why through capitalism liberal democracies more successfully embraced the scientific and technical achievements available in the eighteenth and nineteenth centuries. And he asserted a correlation. Fukuyama insists that the advance of capitalism has been so great that, regardless of the governmental system, this economic system insinuated itself throughout the world and forced rationalizing and improving economic production, thus creating enormous wealth. Fukuyama argued that this discipline and its results were so appealing and successful that all would adopt the practice of liberal democracy. Not only would socialism eventually succumb to this logic, but the appeal of liberal democracy was responsible. Further, legal and political equality brought the end to the combination of masters and dispossessed. If all are, in fact, equal, then enslavement becomes impossible. In his view, democracy itself accelerated mutual understanding, accommodated through political negotiation. The ultimate result of all this would be that states would give up domination over other states and general peace would be achieved.

As many readers know, Fukuyama has modified his views and distanced himself from some former allies, as subsequent events unseated his expectations. But his book remains worthy of consideration because of its iconic status and lingering support in some quarters. In short, the book outlined Fukuyama's commitment to its principles, and many do believe that postliberal revolutions, even if they persist, are at best useless and wasteful. The history recounted in this survey of ideas makes no attempt to judge revolutionaries collectively, but it shows that once the genie was out of the bottle, revolution became a consistent tool to remedy many different problems. The sudden use of religious motivation among the ranks of revolutionaries underscores the pervasiveness of the broad use of the revolutionary concept. It also reveals that despite revolution's many failures and very high costs, some remain optimistic that it will work. In fact, Billington was correct in a limited way that revolution could spread like a fire during some particularly brief time spans: in particular 1830, 1848, 1917, 1968, 1989, and most recently 2010. And who can doubt at this writing that China has, despite serious failings, transformed itself through its communist revolution from what it was a century ago.

As we have seen, the history of revolution casts light on why so fraught an effort continues and proliferates. With far less enthusiasm and greater skepticism about revolution than Fukuyama expressed regarding capitalism, the story told here reveals that the source for revolution lies in the problems and needs that emerge. Revolutionaries generally project laudable goals, at least in the abstract. And many different kinds of revolution will emerge in response to the problems that exist. Even though revolutionary societies are not usually remodeled or even repaired, efforts continue. Revolutions may fail for many reasons: a defective theory of change; failed predictions of future developments; the surprise of revolutionaries about the extent of resistance to the revolution (even though the latter is likely an effect of radical change); the seductive personal opportunities for the revolutionaries; and an insupportable cost in lives and property. But while outside observers decry the effort, the idea of revolution often continues to enjoy support because achievements are measured against previous conditions. In addition, however uncertain the success of a revolution, the belief in perfectibility of humanity, suggested by the philosophes of the eighteenth century, still drives people forward to undertake change and invent new notions of what that change might be.

Notes

Chapter 1

1 Robert R. Palmer, *The Age of the Democratic Revolution, vol. 1 The Struggle, and vol. 2 The Challenge* (Princeton, 1959 and 1964); and Franco Venturi, *The End of the Old Regime in Europe*, 3 vols. (Princeton, 1981).

2 Lynn Hunt, *Inventing Human Rights in History* (New York, 2007).

3 Paul Hazard, *The European Mind* (Cleveland, 1963), p. 13.

4 Ibid., pp. 14, 17.

5 Parlements had to register edicts before they became law. In general, parlements possessed the right to complain formally, and such objections were called remonstrances.

6 In François Furet and Mona Ozouf, eds., *A Critical Dictionary of the French Revolution* (Cambridge, MA, 1989), p. 823.

7 Jack Richard Censer, *Prelude to Power: The Parisian Radical Press, 1789–1791* (Baltimore, 1976), p. 47.

8 Ibid., p. 65.

9 Jeremy Popkin, *You Are All Free: The Haitian Revolution and the Abolition of Slavery* (Cambridge, 2010).

10 Edmund Burke and Thomas Paine, *Reflections on the Revolution in France* and *the Rights of Man* (New York, 1961), p. 45.

11 Ibid., pp. 63, 64.

12 Ibid., p. 104.

13 Ibid., p. 71.

14 Ibid., p. 154.

15 Ibid., pp. 294, 296.

16 Ibid., p. 379.

17 Ibid., p. 383.

18 Ibid., p. 385.

Chapter 2

1 David Bushnell, ed., *El Libertador: Writings of Simón Bolívar* (Oxford, 2003), pp. 38–39.

2 Ibid., p. 38.

3 Ibid., p. 36.

4 Ibid., p. 39.

5 Lloyd Kramer, *Nationalism in Europe and America: Politics, Cultures, and Identities since 1775* (Chapel Hill, 2011), p. 5.

6 Benedict Anderson, *Imagined Communities: Reflections on the Origin and Spread of Nationalism* (New York, 2006).

7 Charles E. Clark, *Public Prints: The Newspaper in Anglo-American Culture, 1665–1740* (Oxford, 1994).

8 Stefano Recchia and Nadia Vrbinati, eds. *A Cosmopolitanism of Nations: Giuseppe Mazzini's Writings on Democracy, Nation Building, and International Relations* (Princeton, 2009), pp. 2–3.

9 Ibid., p. 187.

10 Ibid., p. 194.

11 Ibid., p. 194.

12 Ibid., p. 188.

13 Ibid., p. 238.

14 Ibid., pp. 111–117.

15 Lucy Riall, *Garibaldi: Invention of a Hero* (New Haven, 2007).

16 R.B. Rose, *Gracchus Babeuf: The First Revolutionary Communist* (Stanford, 1978).

17 Karl Marx and Friedrich Engels, *The Communist Manifesto*, ed. Samuel H. Beer (New York, 1955), p. viii.

18 Ibid., p. 21.

19 *Karl Marx: A Nineteenth Century Life* (New York, 2013).

20 *Karl Marx: His Life and Environment*, 4th ed. (Oxford, 1978), p. 181.

21 Marx and Engels, *Communist Manifesto*, passim.

22 Jonathan Sperber, *Karl Marx: A Nineteenth-Century Life* (New York and London, 2013), p. 536.

23 Quoted in David McLellan, *The Thought of Karl Marx* (New York, 1971).

24 Robert C. Tucker, *The Marxian Revolutionary Idea* (New York, 1969), pp. 28–29.

25 Sperber, *Karl Marx*, p. 534.

26 David McLellan, *The Thought of Karl Marx* (New York, 1971), p. 217.

27 English version (New York, 1964).

28 English version (New York, 1975).

29 Alexis de Toqueville, *Recollections*, J.P. Mayer and A.P. Kerr, eds. Translated by George Lawrence (Garden City, NY, 1971).

30 Ibid., p. 15. This was his second most quoted line; the first from the *Communist Manifesto* was "Workers of the world unite: You have nothing to lose but your chains."

31 Ibid., p. 17.

32 Ibid., pp. 18–19.

33 Ibid., pp. 20–21.

34 *Recollections*, p. 168.

35 Ibid., pp. 178–179.

36 Ibid., p. 177.

37 Ibid., p. 181.

38 Ibid., pp. 193–196.

Chapter 3

1 Bertram D. Wolfe, *Three Who Made a Revolution: A Biographical History, 2nd ed.* (New York, 1964), pp. 65–66.

2 *What Is to Be Done? Burning Questions of Our Movement* (New York, 1961).

3 Andrez Mun Walicki, *Marxism and the Leap to the Kingdom of Freedom: The Rise and Fall of the Communist Utopia* (Stanford, 1995), pp. 274–302.

4 Rex A. Wade, *The Russian Revolution* (Cambridge, 2000), p. 274.

5 C. Martin Wilbur, *Sun Yat-sen, Frustrated Patriot* (New York, 1976), pp. 216–17.

6 Lee Feigon, *Chen Duxiu: Founder of the Chinese Communist Party* (Princeton, 1983), p. 152.

7 Ibid.

8 Stuart Schram, *The Thought of Mao Tse-Tung* (Cambridge, 1989), p. 128.

9 Rebecca E. Karl, *Mao Zedong and China in the Twentieth-Century World* (Durham, 2010), passim.

10 Peter Hudis and Kevin B. Anderson, *The Rosa Luxemburg Reader* (New York, 2004), p. 248.

11 Ibid., p. 242.

12 Ibid., p. 243.

13 Ibid., p. 286.

14 Ibid., p. 283.

15 V.I. Lenin, *What Is to Be Done? Burning Questions of Our Movement* (New York, 2005), p. 80.

16 Hudis and Anderson, *Luxemburg Reader*, p. 308.

17 Ibid., p. 309.

18 Ibid., p. 302.

19 Ibid., p. 305.

Chapter 4

1 Vo Nguyen Giap, *People's War, People's Army: The Viet Cong Insurrection Manual for Underdeveloped Countries* (New York, 1962, rev. 1968), pp. 110–11.

2 Ibid., pp. 128–129.

3 Che Guevara, *Guerrilla Warfare* (New York, 1961); and Régis Debray, *Revolution in the Revolution? Armed Struggle and Political Struggle in Latin America*, trans. Bobbye Ortiz (New York, 1967).

4 Guevara, *Guerilla Warfare*, p. 51.

5 Debray, *Revolution in the Revolution?*, p. 105.

6 Ibid., p. 116.

7 Trans. by Constance Farrington (New York, 1963).

8 Published in English by Grove Press (New York) in 1967.

9 Fanon, *Wretched*, pp. 38–39.

10 Ibid., p. 39.

11 Ibid., p. 61.

12 Ibid., p. 95.

13 Ibid., p. 95.

14 Ibid., pp. 108–109.

15 Ibid., p. 130.

16 Ibid., p. 182.

17 Ibid., p. 197.

18 "Islamic Government," in *Islam and Revolution: Writings and Declarations of Iman Khomeini*, trans. by Hamid Algar (Berkeley, 1981), pp. 27–165.

19 Ibid., pp. 90–91.

20 Ibid., p. 142.

21 Ibid., p. 28.

22 Ibid., p. 75.

23 Ibid., p. 147.

24 Ibid., p. 149.

25 Ibid., p. 147.

26 Ibid., p. 138.

27 Ervand Abrahamian, *Khomeinism: Essays on the Islamic Republic* (Berkeley, 1993). See also Shaul Bakhash, *The Reign of the Ayatollahs: Iran and the Islamic Revolution* (New York, 1984).

28 Abrahamian, *Khomeinism*, p. 49.

29 Ibid., pp. 47–49.

Conclusion

1 Keith Baker, "Revolution," in Colin Lucas, ed., *The French Revolution and the Creation of Modern Political Culture*, vol. 2 (Oxford, 1988).

2 For an excellent survey of this work, see Jack Goldstone, "Theories of Revolution: The Third Generation," *World Politics*, vol. 32, no. 3 (April 1980), pp. 425–453. Also "Toward a Fourth Generation of Revolutionary Theory," *Annual Review of Political Science*, vol. 4 (2001), pp. 139–187.

3 Theda Skocpol, *States and Social Revolutions: A Comparative Analysis of France, Russia, and China* (Cambridge, 1979).

4 Used for this analysis is the Norton edition (New York, 1970).

5 See François Furet, *Interpreting the French Revolution*, trans. Elborg Forster (Cambridge, 1981).

6 James Billington, *Fire in the Minds of Men* (New York, 1980).

7 Ibid., p. 5.

8 Francis Fukuyama, *The End of History and the Last Man* (New York, 1992).

Index

Note: Locators with 'n' denote note numbers.